Study Guide

ZAPPING the ACT

Test Preparation for the ACT

Doorway to College™ **Foundation**

Supporting the transition to higher education

ACKNOWLEDGMENTS

Author: Douglas J. Paul, Ph.D.

Editorial Team: Julia Wasson, Karen Nichols, Charles Collins, Gary Hirsch, Terry Meier

Graphic Design: Kelli Cerruto

Cover: Christopher Reese

CONTRIBUTORS

Acknowledgment of Contributions: The presenters of several thousand seminars have contributed their time and energy to the continuing evolution and improvement of this program since its origin in 1985. Special recognition goes to Rick Adler, Diana Anderson, Marty Barrett, Jim Bartlett, Lyn Benedict, Dennis Benson, Carol Braker, Debara Burke, Kaye Byrnes, Joe Carney, Esther Caudle, Henry Caudle, Coral Chilcote, Sheila Cocke, Shari Cornelison, Josh Crittenden, Brian Crouch, Kyra Curtis, Matthew Dahmen, Howard DeWild, Christine Edmunds, Patricia Fremarek, Bob Gould, Sue Grohn, Susan Hamel, Zack Hamingson, Steve Hausauer, Liz Higgins, Gary Hirsch, Pamela Hughes, Clint Huntrods, Marilyn Jackson, Rick Kemmer, Hildred Lewis, Kerri Mabee, Wanda Martinez, Wendy Mattingly, Esther McGuire, Jay Meier, Terry Meier, Dan Mohwinkel, Pat Mooney, Michael Morgan, Deb Oronzio, Jane Petersen, Jim Petersen, Gareth Reagan, Dan Ryan, Kim Stanley, Tom Stirling, Laura Stolpe, Milton Strange, Dan Thorstenson, Linda Usrey, Linda Welp, Audra Yokley.

In addition, guidance officers and administrators in hundreds of school districts have provided data for the research basis of the program strategies and focus. We also thank the more than 500,000 students who have offered their personal evaluation of the seminar and given their comments for areas of weakness and strength.

ABOUT DOORWAY TO COLLEGE FOUNDATION

Doorway to College Foundation strives to demystify the college application process in its many forms. We give parents and students the information needed to be fully informed and prepared for the challenges and changes that lie on the horizon. For more information about Doorway to College Foundation's products and services, visit www.doorwaytocollege.com.

Doorway to College™ Foundation
Supporting the transition to higher education

3106 Rochester Avenue
Iowa City, Iowa 52245
P: 877.928.8378
F: 319.499.5289

Doorway to College   @Doorway2College   Doorway to College   Doorway to College

10 9 8 7 6

ISBN: 978-1-941219-12-6

ZAPS® is a registered trademark of Profiles Corporation. Used by Doorway to College Foundation with specific permission.

Copyright © 2019 Profiles Corporation, Iowa City, Iowa. All Rights Reserved. Licensed to Doorway to College Foundation, 3106 Rochester Avenue, Iowa City, Iowa 52245. Previous editions: 2017, 2016, 2015, 2013, 2011, 2012, 2010, 2009, 2007, 2006, 2004, 2002, 1998, 1992

Table of Contents

How to Use This Book v

Introduction
    What's on the Test? 1
    Take Control of the ACT Test 3
    A Note about Timing 5
    Guessing 6
    ZAPPING 6
    How Does *ZAPPING* Work? 7
    General Tips for the ACT 9
    On Test Day 11

The English Test
    What to Expect 13
    Scoring 14
    Practicing on Your Own 16
    Strategies 17
    Grammar Review 22

The Writing Test
    What to Expect 29
    Scoring 30
    Strategies 32
    Essay Traps 34
    Sample Writing Prompts 35

The Mathematics Test
    What to Expect 39
    Scoring 40
    Practicing on Your Own 42
    A Word About Calculators 43
    Strategies 44
    Error Types 49
    Story Problems 51
    Mathematics Concepts Review 52

The Reading Test
    What to Expect 59
    Scoring 60
    Practicing on Your Own 63
    Strategies 64

The Science Test
    What to Expect 69
    Scoring 70
    Practicing on Your Own 72
    Strategies 73
    Attacking ACT Science Graphs 78

Appendix A 79
    Seminar Pages

Appendix B 83
    Score Conversion Tables

Appendix C 87
    Answer Reviews
        English Workouts 88
        Mathematics Workouts 108
        Reading Workouts 139
        Science Workouts 151

Appendix D 166
    Persuasive Argument Structures 167

> If we did all the things we were capable of doing, we would literally astound ourselves.
> —Thomas Edison

How to Use this Book

Congratulations on taking an important step toward securing your future success! If you are attending a *ZAPS* seminar or webinar from Doorway to College Foundation, your instructor will explain how to use these materials. If you are studying on your own, this page will help you get started. This Study Guide is divided into several sections:

1. Introduction and General Tips
2. English
3. Writing
4. Mathematics
5. Reading
6. Science
7. Appendix A: Seminar pages
8. Appendix B: Scoring information
9. Appendix C: Answer reviews for Workouts
10. Appendix D: Persuasive argument structures

Accompanying this *Study Guide* are 24 practice-test Workouts in four booklets. Each booklet contains six shortened practice tests to use in your seminar or webinar and in your at-home practice. Detailed answer explanations for all the Workouts are included in Appendix C. Below are a few tips to help you get the most out of these study materials.

- **Begin preparing well in advance.** Don't wait until the night before the test.
- **Set aside a few minutes every day to practice.** We recommend 30 minutes each day.
- **Create a personalized study plan.** How you design your study plan will depend on the amount of time you have until the test. Your plan should also account for your personal strengths and weaknesses in the five content areas. A suggested Kick-off Plan is given below.

Kick-Off Plan for Studying on Your Own

Step 1: Read the Introduction and take one English Workout.

Step 2: Read the English tips and review answer explanations for the test you took in Step 1.

Step 3: Take one Math Workout.

Step 4: Review the math tips and answer explanations for the test you took in Step 3.

Step 5: Review the reading tips and take one Reading Workout.

Step 6: Study the answer explanations for the test you took in Step 5.

Step 7: Review the science tips and take one Science Workout.

Step 8: Study the answer explanations for the test you took in Step 7.

Suggestions for focusing your additional practice sessions are given in the "Practicing on Your Own" tips at the beginning of each section of this *Study Guide*.

> The secret of getting ahead is getting started. The secret of getting started is breaking your complex, overwhelming tasks into small, manageable tasks, and then starting on the first one.
> —Mark Twain

Introduction

What's on the Test?

THE ACT ENGLISH TEST
45 minutes   75 questions

Let's take a look . . . Open your copy of the *ZAPPING the ACT: English* Workouts booklet.

This test assesses your knowledge of written English:

- Punctuation
- Grammar
- Sentence structure

} **Usage & Mechanics** (40 items in all)

- Strategy
- Organization
- Style

} **Rhetorical Skills** (35 items in all)

The left column presents a passage—the right column presents questions. For most of the questions, some text is underlined in the passage; you need to choose the correct way to write each underlined part. As you read the passage, you will be considering the different choices. It looks harder than it is.

About two or three questions per passage will be style, organization, or strategy items. For example, look at questions 8 and 25 in English Workout A in your test booklet. These items are sometimes indicated by a special box instead of by an underlined part of the sentence. To answer these types of problems, you need to read the test as if you were editing it.

THE ACT MATHEMATICS TEST
60 minutes   60 questions

Take a look at the *ZAPPING the ACT: Math* Workouts booklet.

This test assesses your ability to solve regular math problems:

- Arithmetic and pre-algebra   12 items
- Elementary algebra   12 items
- Intermediate algebra and coordinate geometry   18 items
- Plane geometry   14 items
- Trigonometry   4 items

The editors at ACT have arranged the math problems in the order that *they* think is from easy to hard. When you take the test, however, you'll find the easy problems mixed in with the hard ones, depending on your strengths and weaknesses.. On the ACT math test, algebra is mixed in with arithmetic and geometry.

If you have taken a regular series of math classes (pre-algebra, algebra I, geometry, algebra II), there shouldn't be more than three or four problems that seem totally over your head.

THE ACT READING TEST
35 minutes   40 questions

Take a look at the *ZAPPING the ACT: Reading* Workouts booklet.

This test assesses your ability to read and answer questions about a passage, such as the following:

- Identify supporting details
- Draw conclusions
- Make comparisons
- Make generalizations

You will read four passages and answer ten questions on each one. One of the passages will be composed of two short selections that are related in some way, and you'll be expected to consider these two selections together in answering a few questions. This test is not much different from all the other standardized reading tests you've taken.

THE ACT SCIENCE TEST
35 minutes   40 questions

Take a look at the *ZAPPING the ACT: Science* Workouts booklet.

This test has some of the features of a reading comprehension test, only with a science angle. Instead of a passage, you will read an "information set" and then answer questions. There are three types of information sets:

- Research summaries (descriptions of experiments and results)

  3 passages with 6 items each

- Data representation (charts with some descriptive text)

  3 passages with 5 items each

- Conflicting viewpoints (reading comprehension, alternative hypotheses or views)

  1 passage with 7 items

THE ACT WRITING TEST (OPTIONAL)

There is also an optional Writing Test (the Essay). You are given a short prompt, and you have to write about one page. No factual information is required. See pages 29–38 for detailed information and practice writing prompts.

Take Control of the ACT

Think of this challenge as a competition. You do not need to let ACT control every aspect of this contest. The more *you* take control, the better chance you have at reaching your highest personal potential.

ACT CONTROLS—

1) Date and location of the test

2) Environment for administration

3) Technical specifications of the test

4) Sequence of test items

5) Raw score (number correct) to ACT score conversion

These five elements are beyond your control. These are the "givens." There are other important elements, however, that you *can* control.

YOU CONTROL—

1) Level and intensity of advance preparation

2) Your personal scoring goals

3) Attack strategy for each subtest

4) Sequence of questions as you choose to answer them

5) Mental attitude before and during the test

> Luck is what happens when preparation meets opportunity.
> —Seneca

Do not surrender control of the factors you *can* control.

GOAL: To help you achieve your highest-possible score on each subtest of the ACT

Your personal "highest-possible score" depends on your academic ability in each subject area tested. When you take the ACT, there are a number of factors that can lower your score. The goal of test preparation is to minimize the effects of those negative factors.

OBJECTIVE 1: To demystify the ACT Test

In order to get your highest possible score on the ACT, you need to know as much as possible about it. In this *Study Guide* and in the accompanying *Workout* booklets, you will be presented with each type of question on the ACT, the difficulty levels you should expect, and the content you need to master in order to do well.

OBJECTIVE 2: To reduce test anxiety and its negative effects on your scores

The ACT is guaranteed to create as much anxiety as possible. Although we can't change the testing situation, we can help you take control of it. These study materials will help you know what to expect so that you will find the situation more familiar. And when the test actually begins, your preparation will reduce overall anxiety. You will be less likely to panic during the test because you will have a variety of strategies to employ when you don't know the answer to a problem.

OBJECTIVE 3: To teach you both general and specific strategies for taking multiple-choice tests

This *Study Guide* covers numerous strategies for taking tests. Some of these methods will become tools that you may apply to any multiple-choice test. Other strategies are specific to the types of items that appear on the ACT.

The emphasis of this book is on what to do when you don't immediately know the correct answer. The main strategy, called *ZAPPING*, teaches you to identify and eliminate incorrect choices before selecting an answer. This strategy is modified slightly for each type of ACT item. *ZAPPING* is a technique you can transfer to every multiple-choice test that you take in high school or college.

Introduction

A Note About Timing

Like many competitive events, all of the ACT subtests are timed. Many students who have the skills necessary to eventually find all of the right answers do poorly only because of a timing problem.

Wear a watch to the test!

The first thing to do at the start of each session is to write down the time that it will end. The people who administer the test (the proctors) are instructed to announce when you have five minutes left. They are also free to write the start and stop time on the board. Don't count on them—they may fail to give you this courtesy. *And don't rely on your memory!*

Many of the test-taking strategies in this book will require you to be aware of the time all the way through the test, not just at the end. We have two recommendations on where to write the time. Take your pick:

- **Our favorite spot:** Write it on the front cover of your test booklet. If you write it somewhere in the middle of the test, you will have to flip to find it. Although you'll need to turn to the cover to see the time, at least you'll be able to do this quickly.

- **The worst choice:** Many students think they will simply remember the stop time. Don't try it. When you are concentrating on the test, it's very difficult to keep timing in mind. Write it down.

At the start of EVERY test, write down the time for completion. This is an easy place to establish control.

Guessing

Never, ever, for any reason, leave any blanks on the ACT. Blind guessing cannot hurt you—it can only help you.

> **If you leave blanks on this test, you are throwing away points.**

Whenever possible, try to eliminate choices *before* you guess. By learning ways to eliminate wrong choices, you can significantly increase your score.

ZAPPING

Zero-in And Pick

Doorway to College Foundation teaches a unique strategy for "zeroing-in" on the right answer before picking. It's called ZAPPING. The exact method of ZAPPING is different for each type of question on the ACT.

For all of the subtests on the ACT:

1) If you know the answer, answer the question.

2) If you don't know the answer, ZAP before you guess.

3) If you can't ZAP, then make a blind guess.

> **When you're blind guessing, do so quickly.**
> **A fast guess is just as good as a slow guess.**

Introduction

How Does *ZAPPING* Work?

The difficulty of multiple-choice tests is not controlled simply by the questions. It is also determined by the wrong answer choices. Three versions of a sample test question will illustrate this point.

Version One: Moderate to hard difficulty

Which president added a corollary to the Monroe Doctrine?
- A. William Henry Harrison
- B. William Howard Taft
- C. Theodore Roosevelt
- D. Woodrow Wilson

Version Two: Changed by an editor to make it easier

Which president added a corollary to the Monroe Doctrine?
- A. Ronald Reagan
- B. Hillary Clinton
- C. Theodore Roosevelt
- D. George W. Bush

Notice that the question in Version Two is the same as in Version One. The correct answer is also the same. The item is easier because more students will be able to eliminate the wrong choices.

Let's take a look at one more revision of this question. Again, notice that the question and correct answer remain the same.

Version Three: Easy

Which president added a corollary to the Monroe Doctrine?
- A. Lady Gaga
- B. Homer Simpson
- C. Theodore Roosevelt
- D. Harry Potter

The point of Version Three is to demonstrate that even a difficult item becomes simple if some of the choices are obviously wrong.

If you can learn ways to make wrong choices in the ACT more obvious, the questions will become easier—*and* your scores will go up.

> **Part of your challenge when you take the ACT is to spot choices that are like Lady Gaga and Harry Potter.**

Multiple-choice items are naturally vulnerable to ZAPPING. We can look at the writing and editorial effort as the process of putting test items together. In the same way, we can think of ZAPPING as taking test items apart.

Some students discover ZAPPING as naturally as learning to walk. If you have always ZAPPED multiple-choice tests, you are starting this program with a serious advantage. The focus now will be to learn specific ZAPPING strategies for each type of question on the ACT.

It is not really possible to construct a machine-scorable multiple-choice test that is completely invulnerable to ZAPPING. Besides, even if the testing companies *could* build an unzappable test, it wouldn't be a good idea.

==ZAPPING allows students to use partial knowledge to eliminate choices.== Therefore, a ZAP-able test may be even better than one that can't be ZAPPED. To the degree that ZAPPING can help students on all multiple-choice tests, the ZAP-ability of the ACT probably contributes to making it a reasonable predictor of success in college.

> **No matter how poorly you guess, any difference will always be in the positive direction. You can't hurt your score by guessing.**

General Tips for the ACT

tip 1 — There is only one correct answer to each item.

The ACT editors try to make sure that every item has one—and only one—correct answer. Even if two answer choices (called "foils" in the testing business) seem okay, there is probably a technical reason why one of those answers is wrong. You might run into this problem with the Reading Test and with the style questions on the English Test. These are the most likely places where some questions will seem to have two correct answers.

Do not waste time thinking about how a second answer could be defended. The ACT editors do not intentionally create two correct answers, and the odds of a student winning an argument with ACT are quite remote. Besides, most people who can argue convincingly in favor of a wrong answer usually know which answer was considered correct in the first place. That is the answer you need to choose to get your best score. Don't waste energy making mental protests while you're taking the test.

tip 2 — Trick questions don't show up on the ACT (not on purpose, anyway).

The editorial staff at ACT tries to spot trick questions before they make it to a final form of the test. Trick questions that get by the editors are nearly always thrown out after a field test. So don't think the test is trying to trick you—not on purpose anyway.

The main point of the ACT is to separate "good" students from "poor" students. Trick questions don't help achieve this goal. Therefore, the ACT editors do not intentionally include trick questions on the test. Keep in mind, however, that anybody can make a mistake, including the people at ACT.

tip 3 — There is no identifiable pattern of correct answers.

The ACT editors are very careful about making sure that the correct answers to their questions do not form a predictable pattern on the answer sheet. Even if there were a predictable pattern, only students achieving a perfect score would be able to discern it accurately. Even if you answered as few as one fourth of the questions wrong, a perfect pattern would look totally random.

Some students look for patterns whenever they run into a guessing situation. "Let's see now," they reason, "I haven't picked a D for about eight or nine questions, so I'll guess D on this one." Sound familiar? Don't waste your time trying to track patterns because there simply aren't any.

tip 4 — All choices are equally likely to occur.

On the tests that your teachers write, choice B or C will probably be correct more often than choices A or D. On the ACT, this idea does not hold true. The ACT editors pay careful attention to the frequency of answers, and they change the order of choices whenever necessary. When you're guessing, the main thing is to move quickly. A fast guess is just as good as a slow guess.

tip 5 — For you as an individual, the difficulty of the items is generally random.

You should always answer the easy questions first and skip over the harder ones. That way, if you need to guess on some items as time is running out, you'll be guessing on the items that are the hardest ones for you. Otherwise, you might end up losing an easy point simply because you didn't attempt all the easy items.

tip 6 — If you take control of the ACT, you are likely to improve your performance.

We've already talked about certain elements of the test that are controlled by ACT and other elements that are under your personal control. You need to control everything you can. Your participation in this program indicates that you have taken a big step in the right direction.

tip 7 — Write freely in your test book and transfer answers carefully.

As you take the test, use *ZAPPING* strategies to cross out obvious wrong answers in your test booklet (not on your answer sheet). Then transfer your chosen answers immediately to the answer sheet. Be extremely careful to code the matching item number.

On Test Day

You need to know in advance the location of your test center. Find out where it is *before* the day of the test. If the location isn't familiar, drive over a day or two before the test. Pay attention to parking options and total travel time. Colleges almost never accept applicants who get hopelessly lost and drive around in circles when they should be taking the ACT. Once you know where the test center is, make sure you get there on time.

Test day is not the time to sleep in or linger over breakfast. Your photo ID is critical. If you don't have a photo ID, you will *not* be admitted even if you happen to know the person checking IDs.

> **On the day of the test, take the following items to the testing site:**
>
> 1. **Your admissions ticket**
> 2. **Your driver's license or picture I.D.**
> 3. **Four sharpened No. 2 lead pencils with erasers**
> 4. **A wristwatch**
> 5. **An approved calculator**

The ACT experience drags on for more than four hours, so make certain you are comfortable when you take it. This is a performance test. You are competing with yourself more than with other students in your class. Just as in sports or arts competitions, your attention and effort on the day of the test may determine whether you attain your personal best. Your score will reflect how you do on one day and one day only.

Your performance on the ACT is important to your future, and you have a right to take it under the best possible conditions. If you are left handed, for example, insist on a left-handed desk. If the sun is in your eyes, ask to close the curtains (before the test begins). If you are distracted by something in the room, do not be afraid to tell the proctors. For example, the person behind you might be coughing or sneezing, or the air conditioner might be blowing in your ear. Most proctors are really very nice people who would be glad to help you if you let them know that you have a problem with the test-taking conditions.

New Readiness Scores & Reporting Categories

When you receive your ACT scores, you will see a lot of information in addition to the composite score and subject area subscores that have traditionally been reported. Here is some of the information you will receive.

Readiness Scores & Score Indicators

The following scores and indicators have been added as of Fall 2015:

- ELA Score (1–36) = Average of English, Reading, and Writing scores; reported only for students taking all three ELA subtests
- STEM Score (1–36) = Average of Math and Science scores
- Understanding Complex Texts (Below Proficient to Above Proficient), showing your "ability to identify the central meaning and purposes of increasingly complex texts"
- Progress Toward Career Readiness (1–36), predicting your performance on another ACT test series, WorkKeys, which measures foundational work skills

Reporting Categories

Beginning in Fall 2016, in addition to the composite score and four subject subscores, students will be given score breakdowns for each subject based on ACT's College Readiness Standards and the Common Core.

What It Means

Here's what these changes mean for you:

- The 1–36 score scale for the subtests and composite score will remain the same.
- While these new scores and reporting categories provide additional information about your performance, *these changes do not affect how you should prepare for the ACT.*

The English Test

What to Expect

For the ACT English Test, you will read five passages that are generally devoid of any interesting content. These passages are full of errors in punctuation, grammar, usage, and sentence structure. Most of the items consist of underlined words, phrases, or sentences. You have to pick, from four choices, the best way to write the underlined part. There are also items that are supposed to measure rhetorical skills, such as strategy, organization, and style. These items contain an underlined phrase or a box with an item number.

In addition to your total English score, your score report will provide two subscores related to the English Test. These scores represent subskills in approximately the following proportions:

- Usage/mechanics
  - Punctuation (10–15%)
  - Grammar and Usage (15–20%)
  - Sentence Structure (20–25%)
- Rhetorical skills
  - Strategy (15–20%)
  - Organization (10–15%)
  - Style (15–20%)

Be prepared to ZAP almost every item.

In terms of test preparation, you can pretty much ignore these subscores. In fact, it's almost impossible to get any meaningful use out of them.

Instead of subscores, pay attention to which items require an understanding of the passage content and which items are dependent only on rules of proper mechanics.

On the ACT, in order to make sure that wrong answers are absolutely wrong, the item writer often is forced to write answer choices (called *foils*) that contain fairly obvious errors. If you are watching for these, this feature of the test gives you a great advantage.

The ACT English Test is constructed in such a way that, quite frequently, it appears that a more difficult question is being asked than is really the case. Additional errors are often introduced in the foils. The additional errors are many times easier to spot than the original difficult answer.

Scoring

What does it take to achieve your personal best on the ACT English Test?

The tables on the following page are based on a few assumptions:

1. You will correctly answer the questions that you know for sure. (The tables make no allowance for marking errors on the answer sheet.)

2. You will blind guess or *ZAP* the questions you don't know the answers to. (You should leave no blanks.)

3. The raw scores on the tables (number of questions answered correctly) reflect the average results of guessing. For example, if you blind guessed on 12 questions with a one out of four chance, your expected gain would be three points. In actual practice you might pick up more or fewer points.

For purposes of illustration, let's assume that a student named Shanti knows 25 questions for sure and blind guesses on the other 50 questions. The average pickup from guessing would be 12.5, so Shanti's Raw Score would be 38 (25 + 12.5 = 37.5). This converts to an ACT score of 15. (See the conversion table on page 84.)

With *ZAPPING*, however, Shanti could increase her Raw Score an additional four to 12 points, converting to an ACT score as high as 19. The illustration demonstrates that with Shanti's particular level of English skills, the ACT score could range anywhere from 15 to 19, depending on the application of *ZAPPING* techniques.

The "know for sure" box is an indication of your confident skill level. Use the score conversion table on page 84 to fill in the ACT scores. Notice that *ZAPPING* increases your score no matter where you start on the "know-for-sure" index.

Any particular ability level could yield a range of ACT scores. Your goal is to hit the top of your personal range. Be realistic, but don't settle for 24 if you could hit 27. And don't settle for 27 if you could hit 29.

> When I worked on my game, that's what I thought about. When it happened, I set another goal, a reasonable, manageable goal that I could realistically achieve if I worked hard enough. I guess I approached it with the end in mind. I knew exactly where I wanted to go, and I focused on getting there.
> —Michael Jordan

The English Test

ACT English Test

KNOW 20 for sure	55 UNKNOWNS		
Strategy	If Blind Guess All	If ZAP 1 Foil All	If ZAP 2 Foils All
Guess Yield	14	18	28
Raw Score	34	38	48
ACT Score*			

KNOW 25 for sure	50 UNKNOWNS		
Strategy	If Blind Guess All	If ZAP 1 Foil All	If ZAP 2 Foils All
Guess Yield	13	17	25
Raw Score	38	42	50
ACT Score*	15		19

KNOW 30 for sure	45 UNKNOWNS		
Strategy	If Blind Guess All	If ZAP 1 Foil All	If ZAP 2 Foils All
Guess Yield	11	15	23
Raw Score	41	45	53
ACT Score*			

KNOW 35 for sure	40 UNKNOWNS		
Strategy	If Blind Guess All	If ZAP 1 Foil All	If ZAP 2 Foils All
Guess Yield	10	13	20
Raw Score	45	48	55
ACT Score*			

KNOW 40 for sure	35 UNKNOWNS		
Strategy	If Blind Guess All	If ZAP 1 Foil All	If ZAP 2 Foils All
Guess Yield	9	12	18
Raw Score	49	52	58
ACT Score*			

KNOW 45 for sure	30 UNKNOWNS		
Strategy	If Blind Guess All	If ZAP 1 Foil All	If ZAP 2 Foils All
Guess Yield	8	10	15
Raw Score	53	55	60
ACT Score*			

KNOW 50 for sure	25 UNKNOWNS		
Strategy	If Blind Guess All	If ZAP 1 Foil All	If ZAP 2 Foils All
Guess Yield	6	8	13
Raw Score	56	58	63
ACT Score*			

KNOW 55 for sure	20 UNKNOWNS		
Strategy	If Blind Guess All	If ZAP 1 Foil All	If ZAP 2 Foils All
Guess Yield	5	7	10
Raw Score	60	62	65
ACT Score*			

KNOW 60 for sure	15 UNKNOWNS		
Strategy	If Blind Guess All	If ZAP 1 Foil All	If ZAP 2 Foils All
Guess Yield	4	5	8
Raw Score	64	65	68
ACT Score*			

KNOW 65 for sure	10 UNKNOWNS		
Strategy	If Blind Guess All	If ZAP 1 Foil All	If ZAP 2 Foils All
Guess Yield	3	3	5
Raw Score	68	68	70
ACT Score*			

*The conversion of Raw Score to ACT Score will vary slightly depending on which form of the test you happen to take. The conversion is a statistical adjustment that makes up for the unavoidable differences in the difficulty of the reading passages and test questions.

Practicing on Your Own

Use the following tips to prepare for the ACT English Test:

1. **Do a reality check.**
   Complete one English Workout and determine your score using the appropriate answer key in Appendix C. As you take the test, put a star next to each item that you know for sure.

2. **Refresh your memory**.
   Study pages 17–28 in this *Study Guide*.

   Starting Score _____

3. **Continue working on only one Workout at a time.**
   Don't try to work all of the Workouts in one sitting.
   You will get sick of it and never want to look at the ACT again. It is better to do a little bit every day over a long period than to do one or two marathon sessions.

4. **Don't worry about your score or about timing yourself.**
   First build your skills, then work on your speed. Use the Workout as a diagnostic tool—to find out what types of questions you are missing most and where you need to brush up. Your score will take care of itself.

5. **Study your mistakes**.
   Look up each item you missed in the answer reviews in Appendix C. Make sure you understand why the correct answer is correct and why the wrong choices are wrong. If you are still unclear about a question after reading the answer reviews, mark that question and discuss it with one of your English teachers.

6. **Analyze your errors.**
   Are you missing mostly grammar and punctuation items (commas, semicolons, subject-verb agreement, etc.)? Or are you missing mostly style questions—like the box questions? As you are going over your answers, keep a tally of the types of questions you are missing most, then use that information to design your own study plan.

   If you're rusty on grammar and punctuation, begin by reading the answer reviews for the questions you missed. Then read through the brief grammar review on pages 22 through 28. If you are still foggy on a few of the concepts, ask a teacher to go over them with you.

   If style questions are your problem, the answer reviews will be a big help. Study the wrong choices, even on the questions you got correct. What makes the wrong choices attractive? Try to get inside the test writer's mind and see how these items are being written. Also, discuss some of the style questions with a teacher or friend.

7. **Practice.**
   Complete the English Test in the ACT registration packet available *free* in your guidance office and online at www.actstudent.org.

   Updated Score _____

8. **Change it up.**
   Try a different approach with the online *ZAPS* ACT-Practice Test. Find out more at **www.doorwaytocollege.com/online-act-practice-test**.

The English Test

Strategies

Specific tips for attacking the English Test follow. As you encounter examples of each tip in your practice, write the test item numbers in the boxes provided.

tip 1 — Watch and look out for redundancy. If it can be said with one single word, two words should not be used and applied.

Redundancy is a big deal on the ACT, partly because it is a common problem in the writing of high school and college students. The ACT will often present two words where one will suffice. Three examples of redundancy can be found in the boldfaced statement of the tip above. Circle them.

The English Test likes to underline phrases such as "After they had built and constructed the doghouse" or "It was her first initial appearance." ACT will not make you choose between the two redundant words. They will simply give you a choice that contains only one of those words.

Examples of redundancy

tip 2 — Watch out for sentence fragments.

The ACT will *never* present a sentence fragment as the correct answer choice. (If you don't know the difference between a complete sentence and a fragment, learn it. You need to know.) You'll need to check for fragments whenever you see either—

- a **period** in the underlined part, or
- a **period** in the answer choices.

These are two places where a test editor is likely to place a fragment. Whenever you see a period underlined, check both the preceding and the following sentences to make sure they are both complete. Also, if you can't use a period, you can't substitute a semicolon.

Fragments are Homer Simpson choices. Every time you discover a fragment, you can immediately ZAP "NO CHANGE." The second part of this tip is to always check your answer to make sure your choice does not create a new fragment.

Examples of fragments

tip 3 — When you can't decide between two or three choices, choose the shorter option.

Use this tip only when guessing.

ACT includes many items that ask, "What is the best way to say what is meant?" Their challenge in designing these items is to include attractive wrong choices that don't all stand out like Homer Simpson or Lady Gaga. ACT often makes the wrong choices wrong by making them awkward and wordy.

Whenever you can't decide between two choices, you can ZAP the longer choice and pick the shorter choice. This tip *does not* mean that the shortest choice is *always* the right answer. Apply this idea only after ZAPPING for other reasons. When you get to the point where you need to guess, pick the shortest choice remaining.

Examples of shorter-is-better

tip 4 — Pay careful attention to the context in which an item appears. You can't always read just the underlined parts.

You can assume that everything that is *not* underlined on the ACT English Test is correct. In many instances, an incorrect response is incorrect because it does not work in the context in which it appears. For this reason, it is important to carefully read the sentence or phrase preceding and following the underlined part.

Examples of critical context

tip 5 — Do not be afraid to choose the NO CHANGE option.

The correct answer to a question is not necessarily one that has changed anything. All underline questions and some editing questions offer you NO CHANGE as an answer choice. Do not overlook NO CHANGE as a possible answer to the problem. It will be correct approximately 20 percent of the time it is offered.

Examples of NO CHANGE questions

The English Test

tip 6 — On many items, you can ZAP choices "by ear."

Take the following sentence, for example: *"He seen the handwriting on the wall."* You probably know that "He seen" is inappropriate for the ACT, even if you don't know the grammatical rule. If something *sounds* wrong, it probably *is* wrong.

On the ACT, if you don't immediately know an answer, verbalize the choices in your mind. If an answer choice sounds awkward, it's probably wrong—ZAP it. Your ability to sound out the right answer can be improved with practice. The sample tests should give you an indication of how good an ear you have for this technique.

Examples of ZAPPING by ear

tip 7 — All questions are of equal value, but some question types will cost you a lot more time.

On the English test, some questions are more complicated than a simple redundancy or sentence fragment question. For instance, ACT will occasionally ask you to add a sentence to a passage at a specific point labeled "Point A," "Point B," "Point C," or "Point D." Here's an example:

45. The writer is considering adding the following sentence to the essay:

    When the Department of Defense was created following World War II, the Cabinet position of "Secretary of War" was retired.

    If the writer were to add this sentence to the essay, it would most logically be placed at:
    F. Point A in Paragraph 1.
    G. Point B in Paragraph 3.
    H. Point C in Paragraph 3.
    J. Point D in Paragraph 5.

The points can appear anywhere in the passage and are labeled by bracketed letters, like this: [A].

ACT helps you by telling you the paragraph in which each point can be found, but they can still be a bit hard to spot, so look carefully. At each point, re-read to see whether the sentence to be added is a logical fit with the topic under discussion. If it isn't, ZAP the choice.

Because you have to hunt for the points and re-read sections of the passage, these questions can be a bit time-consuming. If you are running out of time, take a guess and move on. It's only one question out of 75 on the test. In the time you take to answer a question like this, you could probably pick up two — or even three — easier points.

If you choose to skip items like these and come back to them, let the five-minute warning be your reminder to return to them. Leaving a blank on this question — or any other question — is not an option.

tip 8 — Study and compare the choices to avoid creating a new error as you correct the original error.

Often an attractive answer choice will introduce a change in punctuation or usage that makes the choice incorrect. This will be a problem if you don't double-check each question. After you think you see the correct answer, check the other choices to see if another answer is similar. If so, look for the difference between the two choices and reconsider which one is correct.

Examples of *ZAPPING* to avoid creating new errors

tip 9 — For all underlined items, reread the sentence after you plug in your choices.

This is a safety step to avoid making stupid mistakes. It must be done quickly or it can cause problems with your pacing. The best thing to help increase your speed at this is to practice prior to the real test.

tip 10 — When the question number is in a little box, attack it in two steps.

The answers to these box questions often seem arbitrary and vague. You might find two or three choices that look sensible, or you might go through and *ZAP all four* choices as stupid.

Attack Step 1: Determine where in the passage you'll find the answer.

The box questions are based either on a nearby sentence or paragraph, or on the entire passage. Read the question carefully to decide which type it is.

Examples of box questions based on a nearby sentence or paragraph

The Writing Test

What to Expect

ACT's Writing Test is an optional essay based on a single prompt. Some colleges and universities require it for admissions and/or placement purposes, while others do not. When you know which colleges you want to apply to, go to their admissions websites to find out whether they require, recommend, or do not need the Writing Test score.

Even if the colleges on your list don't require the Writing Test, or if you don't yet know which colleges you'll apply to, it is a good idea to take the essay just in case you later decide to attend a college where it is required.

A Three-Part Prompt

You'll be given 40 minutes to study a writing assignment and complete a short, written essay. Your essay will be based on a single prompt that discusses a complex issue. The prompt will have three parts:

- The issue
- Three perspectives on the issue
- The writing task

The first part of the prompt presents a mildly controversial issue with context. This information will be in the form of a single paragraph.

Next, you will see three perspectives on the issue. One is likely to be positive, one negative, and the third could go either way.

Lastly, you will see the writing task itself. It will ask you to evaluate three perspectives on the issue and generate an argument from your own perspective "based on reasoning, knowledge, and experience."

You will also be given two pages of planning space that include a set of guiding questions to help you generate and develop your ideas. These questions are likely to be the same on all forms of the test; to save time on test day, know them before you go.

Your response may agree with any of the three given perspectives wholly or in part, or your own perspective might be completely different. It doesn't matter which side you choose. ACT will not award more points for one opinion over the other.

Look for sample prompts beginning on page 35 of this workbook.

Scoring

If you take the Writing Test, you will receive several scores:

- A single Writing score on a scale of 2 to 12. This score will be the average of the subscores described in next bullet.
- Four subscores between 2 and 12 for each of the Four Domains of Writing Competency (see below).
- An English Language Arts (ELA) score from 1 to 36. This is the average of the English, Reading, and Writing scores for those who take all three of these subtests.

Because it is optional, the Writing Test does not affect your overall composite score.

Four Domains of Writing Competency

The Enhanced Writing Test gives you a chance to demonstrate your writing ability in what ACT calls the Four Domains of Writing Competency:

- Ideas and Analysis
    - Understand an issue and its context well
    - Generate strong ideas in response
    - Demonstrate critical thinking
    - Analyze and evaluate multiple perspectives on a topic
    - Use an effective writing strategy
- Development and Support
    - Illustrate, explain, and support your ideas
    - Use persuasive details and examples based on reasoning, knowledge, and experience
- Organization
    - Organize your argument logically, strategically, and clearly
- Language Use and Conventions
    - Use standard written English (grammar, syntax, word usage, and mechanics)
    - Use a voice and tone suitable to the audience and purpose
    - Express nuanced ideas with precise word choice

Writing Checklist

The following checklist is based on The ACT's Writing Test Scoring Rubric. To earn your highest possible score on the ACT Writing Test, make sure your writing does the following:

Ideas and Analysis

- [ ] The argument engages with multiple perspectives on the issue.
- [ ] The thesis is nuanced and precise in thought and purpose.
- [ ] The argument analyzes the issue and related perspectives within an insightful context.
- [ ] Implications, complexities, tensions, and/or underlying values/assumptions are analyzed and examined.

Development and Support

- [ ] The ideas and claims are well developed and supported, deepening insight into the issue and widening its context.
- [ ] The line of reasoning and illustration is skillful, well-connected, and effective.
- [ ] The supporting details and reasoning show the significance of the argument.
- [ ] Ideas and analysis are supported and enriched by qualifications and complications.

Organization

- [ ] The response is skillfully organized.
- [ ] The writing is unified by a main idea/purpose.
- [ ] The ideas progress logically and improve the effectiveness of the argument.
- [ ] The relationships among ideas are strengthened by transitions between and within paragraphs.

Language Use

- [ ] The argument is enhanced by language via—
  - [ ] Skillful and precise word choice
  - [ ] Varied and clear sentence structure
  - [ ] Strategic and effective style choices, including voice and tone
- [ ] Minor grammar, usage, or mechanics errors do not hinder understanding.

Writing Strategies

We recommend that you approach the Writing Test with a three-step attack plan based on the stages of the writing process.

Step 1: Plan

Step 1 is the most important. Spend about 10 minutes on this step. If you plan well, the actual writing should go quickly.

- **Analyze the prompt.** Expect the prompt to contain the following elements: the topic, examples, the controversy in the form of a question, and a hint at the writing task. Feel free to mark up the prompt as you read, and jot down any ideas that pop into your mind as you go.

- **Evaluate the perspectives.** Expect to see one positive viewpoint, one negative viewpoint, and a third viewpoint that could go either way. Try to summarize each perspective into a single sentence in your mind. Again, take notes as you read, marking ideas you agree or disagree with and jotting down ideas as they come to mind.

- **Analyze the writing task.** The actual writing task will likely be very similar to those given in the sample prompts in this book. Only the topic will change.

- **Draft a thesis statement.** In a single sentence, state your position on the issue. Your position may be the same as, or in partial agreement with, one of the three perspectives, or it may be all your own.

- **Generate ideas.** Explain the relationship between your perspective and the given perspectives. Generate plenty of specific reasons to back up your general statements. You can use evidence (facts, experience, authority), logical reasoning, and emotional appeals. There are several ways to generate ideas, including free-writing, listing, brainstorming, and clustering. Use the approach that works best for you. The work you do on the planning pages won't be scored.

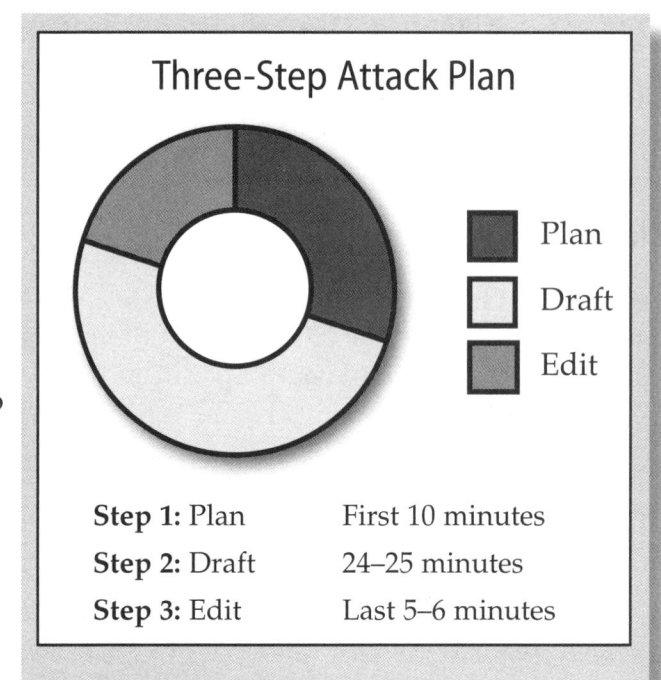

Three-Step Attack Plan

- Plan
- Draft
- Edit

Step 1: Plan — First 10 minutes
Step 2: Draft — 24–25 minutes
Step 3: Edit — Last 5–6 minutes

Key Terms

Here are a few important words you are likely to see in the ACT Writing prompt:

Unified – to unite into a whole

Coherent – well-ordered, understandable

Evaluate – to judge the value or quality of

Perspective – viewpoint

Analyze – to closely and carefully examine the parts of

State – to express

Develop – to make clear through elaboration and detail

Traits of a Strong Thesis Statement

- Takes a clear stand on the issue
- Directly answers the question being asked
- Is more than just an observation; it justifies a discussion by making a claim that others might disagree with
- Is specific
- Can usually be stated in a single sentence

The Writing Test

- **Organize your ideas.** Some students prefer to stick to the traditional five-paragraph essay format. Others want to try a different approach. It's fine to get creative, as long as you fulfill the assignment. The test writers are hoping students will not be afraid to step away from formulaic writing and really show their skills. Check Appendix D of this workbook for a few possible organizational structures.

Following the writing prompt, the ACT will give you two planning pages and a series of guiding questions to help you consider your perspective on the prompt and develop your response. These guiding questions will be very similar to the ones you see below and are expected to be the same on every form of the test. Know them before you go.

> **Guiding Questions**
>
> As you generate ideas and plan your essay, consider the following questions, which are designed to help you think critically about the task:
>
> Strengths and weaknesses of the three perspectives
> - What insights do they give? What do they fail to take into account?
> - Why might they be or not be persuasive to readers?
>
> Your knowledge, values, and experience
> - What is your point of view on this issue? What are the strengths and weaknesses of your viewpoint?
> - How will you back up your viewpoint in your writing?

Step 2: Draft

This is where you put your ideas into sentences and paragraphs on paper. Spend about 24 or 25 minutes drafting your essay. As you write, keep these tips in mind:

- Use appropriate paragraphing.
- Use effective transitions to show the connections among ideas.
- Maintain focus on the thesis and purpose.
- Use a variety of sentence structures.
- Use precise and varied vocabulary.
- Use a voice and tone that are appropriate for the audience and purpose.
- Plan to finish drafting with five to six minutes remaining to polish your work.

Step 3: Edit

With five to six minutes remaining, quickly read over your essay from the perspective of your reader.

- Does the writing take a clear stand on the issue?
- Is there a clear thesis?
- Does the writing consider all three perspectives?
- Is the thesis supported with insightful reasons?
- Does the writing stay focused on the topic?
- Are the ideas logically organized and clearly presented?
- Does the writing thoroughly address the assignment?
- Are the voice and tone appropriate?
- Does the writing use a variety of vocabulary and sentence structures?
- Is it free of errors in grammar, spelling, and usage?
- Is the writing legible (readable)?

Final Tips

You can avoid some of the most common and predictable errors by doing the following in your essay:

- Reread the prompt as you are writing to make sure you're staying on target.
- State your position or thesis statement before giving examples.
- Choose one side of the issue and stick with it; you won't gain points with a wishy-washy position on the issue.
- Use normal handwriting, not too small to easily read and not so large that you seem to be trying to fill the space without writing solid content.
- Provide supporting examples and details to back up your position.
- Make sure your examples relate to your supporting points.
- Write a final paragraph that sums up your position.
- Make sure that your final paragraph is aligned with your thesis statement.

Proofreading Marks

If a teacher, parent, or friend evaluates your practice essays, ask them to use these proofreader's marks to show you how to improve. On test day, use these marks to make changes during the editing stage, as needed. The scorers won't expect your essay to be a perfectly finished product; they will judge it as a draft. But try to present a copy that is as clean and polished as possible within the time available. It is okay to erase, add, subtract, and reorder text as long as your writing is legible, easy to follow, and stays within the body of the essay — not in the margins.

⌒	Delete
⌒	Close up space
⌒	Delete and close up
∧	Insert text
#	Insert space
stet	Let stand
tr ⌒	Transpose
¶	Begin new paragraph
no ¶	No new paragraph
cap	Set in CAPITALS
lc	Lowercase
∧	Comma
∨	Apostrophe or single quote marks
⊙	Period
sp	Spell out

Sample Writing Prompts

Practice Prompt 1

Social Media

Social media use has grown dramatically in the past decade, with three-quarters of all adults now saying they participate in online social networks, up 26% from 2008. People use social media to connect with friends and family locally and across great distances. Users educate themselves by following and interacting with others who share their interests. And social media is used to rapidly spread information, with more than 50% of people saying they have learned about breaking news via social networks. Social media has made this a more connected world, but what is lost when much of our human connection is virtual? Given the growing prevalence of social media, it is worth examining the implications and meaning of its presence in our lives.

Consider the following perspectives, which suggest viewpoints about social media.

Perspective One	Perspective Two	Perspective Three
Social media separates and isolates us as it encourages us to spend more time online. It distracts our attention from work, school, and those who are physically present in our lives. It feeds conflict and division, as we find it easier to say negative things online that we would never say to someone in person.	Social media facilitates human connection and cooperation. We can use it to quickly share information and ideas across the globe, and to band together with likeminded people to support causes we believe in. People also use social media to facilitate face-to-face connections and organize real-life events.	Social media offers powerful and infinite new ways for us to connect and interact. This is good in that it challenges us to imagine how we can use it to better society and to make choices about how we allow its presence into our lives.

Writing Task

Write a unified, coherent essay in which you evaluate multiple perspectives on social media. Be sure to do the following:

- analyze and evaluate each of the given viewpoints

- state and develop your own point of view on the issue

- explain the relationship between your viewpoint and the given viewpoints

Your stance may be in full agreement with any of the others, in partial agreement, or completely different. Support your ideas with reasoning and persuasive details and examples.

Practice Prompt 2

Mandating Healthy Behaviors

For the past several years, organizations and governments have sought to improve human health by decreasing the ease or attractiveness of unhealthy lifestyle choices. Some nations, states, and cities have banned or are considering banning certain types of fats from being used in restaurant foods. Many school districts no longer allow unhealthy foods to be sold on school property via drink and snack machines or fundraisers, or to be used as rewards or special treats in the classroom. Some businesses will no longer hire job applicants with unhealthy habits such as smoking. Measures taken to improve health are considered good for society, but should freedom of choice be taken away in such matters? Given the growing movement to mandate healthy behavior, it is worth examining the implications these rules have on our lives.

Consider the following perspectives, which suggest viewpoints about mandating healthy behaviors.

Perspective One	Perspective Two	Perspective Three
Unhealthy behaviors increase overall health costs for businesses, governments, and individuals and are a drain on our workforce and economy. Businesses and governments have a right and duty to pass health mandates that improve the economic and general well-being of citizens and workers.	Health mandates take away freedom of choice over some of our most personal decisions. People have different diets for all sorts of reasons, including cultural, religious, and economic ones. Governments, businesses, and other institutions should respect individual freedom and not go further than recommending healthy lifestyle choices.	Businesses and other organizations should be free to make their own choices about what products to make or serve, whom to hire, and what rules to set for employees. Governments can encourage healthy choices in positive ways by offering tax incentives and other rewards to organizations and individuals who promote healthy lifestyles.

Writing Task

Write a unified, coherent essay evaluating multiple viewpoints on mandating healthy behaviors. Be sure to do the following:

- analyze and evaluate each of the given viewpoints
- state and develop your own point of view on the issue
- explain the relationship between your viewpoint and the given viewpoints

Your stance may be in full agreement with any of the others, in partial agreement, or completely different. Support your ideas with reasoning and persuasive details and examples.

Practice Prompt 3

Behavior-Tracking Technology

Individual behavior is increasingly monitored by technology called behavior learning or behavior tracking. Retailers recommend products and provide coupons to consumers based on past purchasing habits. Internet users see advertisements relevant to their lives, based on their online behavior. Social media and online media outlets present viewers with news and entertainment based on their interests. Behavior tracking is generally seen as a technological advancement, but are there dangers inherent in such data gathering? Given how the mining of "big data" is accelerating, it is worth considering the implications of behavior tracking on our lives.

Consider the following perspectives, which suggest viewpoints about behavior-tracking technology.

Perspective One	Perspective Two	Perspective Three
Behavior tracking is an invasion of privacy. Data is often gathered about customers without their consent. Such data may one day be used against us in ways we have not yet imagined.	Behavior tracking allows businesses and other organizations to better serve consumers. People can more easily learn about ideas, products, and services that can improve their lives. Such individualization provides better consumer experiences for everyone.	Behavior tracking opens up new possibilities for technology to improve our lives. This challenges us to think about what is possible while also adapting our laws and technologies to protect our freedom and privacy.

Writing Task

Write a unified, coherent essay evaluating multiple viewpoints on behavior-tracking technology. Be sure to do the following:

- analyze and evaluate each of the given viewpoints
- state and develop your own point of view on the issue
- explain the relationship between your viewpoint and the given viewpoints

Your stance may be in full agreement with any of the others, in partial agreement, or completely different. Support your ideas with reasoning and persuasive details and examples.

Practice Prompt 4

Standardized Testing

For several decades, standardized testing has played a large role in K–12 education in the United States. Schools and districts use testing data to measure the effectiveness of their curricula and adjust their teaching accordingly. Students can see how their achievement levels compare to national averages based on a common list of knowledge and skills. Testing data can guide teachers in meeting the needs of individual students according to their academic strengths and weaknesses. Educational data is considered important to teaching and learning, but what are the downsides? Given the increasing role of assessment in education, it is worth examining the implications of its use in our schools.

Consider the following perspectives, which suggest viewpoints about standardized testing in education.

Perspective One	Perspective Two	Perspective Three
Standardized testing is an essential component of good educational practice. Fair, reliable, and objective data is needed to judge the quality of teachers and schools, and to improve teaching and curricula. Standardized tests help to focus teaching on knowledge and skills that all students need to acquire.	Standardized testing is being overused in schools today. Because high stakes for teachers and schools are attached to the test scores, teachers are often pressured to teach to the test. This narrows the curriculum and decreases opportunities for creative, individualized learning.	Standardized tests are just one tool in the educator's toolbox. Whether they are good or bad depends on how they are used. Educational assessment is most useful when it is not attached to rewards or punishments for teachers and schools.

Writing Task

Write a unified, coherent essay evaluating multiple viewpoints on standardized testing in education. Be sure to do the following:

- analyze and evaluate each of the given viewpoints
- state and develop your own point of view on the issue
- explain the relationship between your viewpoint and the given viewpoints

Your stance may be in full agreement with any of the others, in partial agreement, or completely different. Support your ideas with reasoning and persuasive details and examples.

The Mathematics Test

What to Expect

You get to solve 60 problems in 60 minutes. Are you ready? Don't worry. These are totally ordinary problems. Most of them will be fairly easy if you've completed at least one algebra class. And you don't need to get them all right to get a high ACT score. Even if you miss half of the items, you may still score around a 20. Think about that. A score of 50% on a classroom test would usually yield an F. But on the ACT, 50% is right at the national average. So don't think of this test the way you think of a classroom test.

Five content areas are included on the ACT Math Test. These are listed on page 1 of this *Study Guide*. You don't need to memorize any complex formulas, and the test does not require a lot of computation.

In addition to your total math score, your score report will provide three subscores related to the ACT Math Test:

- Pre-algebra/elementary algebra
- Intermediate algebra/coordinate geometry
- Plane geometry/trigonometry

If these categories seem arbitrary to you, it's because they are. The subscores will be of little or no value in terms of preparing for the test. Just as with English, it is highly unlikely that anyone in the universe will care about any of your scores except your total.

Why Study for the Math Test?

If one hundred students with equal math ability were to take the ACT next Saturday, they would not all get the same score. Why? Because the test is not a perfect measure of math ability. A lot of the score has to do with how good you are at taking tests. And some of the score has to do with whether you're having a good or bad day. Preparation and practice can help you achieve a better score than unprepared students who have equal or superior math ability. On the other hand, if you don't practice in advance, you could score worse than some students who aren't as good as you in real math classes.

Scoring

What does it take to achieve your personal best on the ACT Mathematics Test?

The following tables are based on a few assumptions:

1) You will correctly answer the problems that you know for sure. (The tables make no allowance for answer sheet marking errors.)

2) You will blind guess or *ZAP* the unknown problems. (You should leave no blanks.)

3) The raw scores on the tables (number of problems answered correctly) reflect the average results of guessing. For example, if you blind guessed on 15 questions with a one out of five chance, your expected gain would be three points. In actual practice, you might pick up more or fewer points.

For purposes of illustration, let's assume that our friend Shanti knows 35 questions for sure, and blind guesses on the other 25 questions. The average pickup from guessing would be five, so Shanti's Raw Score would be 40 (35 + 5). This converts to an ACT score of 24. (See the conversion table on page 84.)

With *ZAPPING*, however, Shanti could raise her Raw Score as much as eight more points, converting to an ACT score as high as 27. The illustration demonstrates that with Shanti's particular level of math ability, the ACT score could range anywhere from 24 to 27, depending on the application of *ZAPPING* techniques.

The "know for sure" box is an indication of your confident skill level. Use the score conversion table on page 84 to fill in the ACT scores. Notice that *ZAPPING* increases your score no matter where you start on the "know-for-sure" index.

Any particular ability level could yield a range of ACT scores. Your goal is to hit the top of your personal range. Be realistic, but don't settle for 20 if you could hit 24. And don't settle for 24 if you could hit 28.

> There has to be a mathematical explanation for how bad that tie is.
> —Russell Crowe in *A Beautiful Mind*

The Mathematics Test

ACT Mathematics Test

KNOW 10 for sure	50 UNKNOWNS			
Strategy	If Blind Guess All	If ZAP 1 Foil All	If ZAP 2 Foils All	If ZAP 3 Foils All
Guess Yield	10	13	17	25
Raw Score	20	23	27	35
ACT Score*				

KNOW 15 for sure	45 UNKNOWNS			
Strategy	If Blind Guess All	If ZAP 1 Foil All	If ZAP 2 Foils All	If ZAP 3 Foils All
Guess Yield	9	11	15	23
Raw Score	24	26	30	38
ACT Score*				

KNOW 20 for sure	40 UNKNOWNS			
Strategy	If Blind Guess All	If ZAP 1 Foil All	If ZAP 2 Foils All	If ZAP 3 Foils All
Guess Yield	8	10	13	20
Raw Score	28	30	33	40
ACT Score*				

KNOW 25 for sure	35 UNKNOWNS			
Strategy	If Blind Guess All	If ZAP 1 Foil All	If ZAP 2 Foils All	If ZAP 3 Foils All
Guess Yield	7	9	12	18
Raw Score	32	34	37	43
ACT Score*				

KNOW 30 for sure	30 UNKNOWNS			
Strategy	If Blind Guess All	If ZAP 1 Foil All	If ZAP 2 Foils All	If ZAP 3 Foils All
Guess Yield	6	8	10	15
Raw Score	36	38	40	45
ACT Score*				

KNOW 35 for sure	25 UNKNOWNS			
Strategy	If Blind Guess All	If ZAP 1 Foil All	If ZAP 2 Foils All	If ZAP 3 Foils All
Guess Yield	5	6	8	13
Raw Score	40	41	43	48
ACT Score*	24			27

KNOW 40 for sure	20 UNKNOWNS			
Strategy	If Blind Guess All	If ZAP 1 Foil All	If ZAP 2 Foils All	If ZAP 3 Foils All
Guess Yield	4	5	7	10
Raw Score	44	45	47	50
ACT Score*				

KNOW 45 for sure	15 UNKNOWNS			
Strategy	If Blind Guess All	If ZAP 1 Foil All	If ZAP 2 Foils All	If ZAP 3 Foils All
Guess Yield	3	4	5	8
Raw Score	48	49	50	53
ACT Score*				

KNOW 50 for sure	10 UNKNOWNS			
Strategy	If Blind Guess All	If ZAP 1 Foil All	If ZAP 2 Foils All	If ZAP 3 Foils All
Guess Yield	2	3	3	5
Raw Score	52	53	53	55
ACT Score*				

KNOW 55 for sure	5 UNKNOWNS			
Strategy	If Blind Guess All	If ZAP 1 Foil All	If ZAP 2 Foils All	If ZAP 3 Foils All
Guess Yield	1	1	2	3
Raw Score	56	56	57	58
ACT Score*				

*The conversion of Raw Score to ACT Score will vary slightly depending on which form of the test you happen to take. The conversion is a statistical adjustment that makes up for the unavoidable differences in the difficulty of any particular set of math problems.

Practicing on Your Own

Use the following tips to prepare for the ACT Math Test:

1. **Do a reality check.**
   Complete one Mathematics Workout and determine your score using the answer key in Appendix C. As you take the test, put a star next to each problem that you know for sure.

   | Starting Score _____ |

2. **Refresh your memory.**
   Study pages 44–58 in this *Study Guide*.

3. **Continue working only one Workout at a time.**
   Don't try to work all of the Workouts in one sitting.

4. **Don't worry about your score or about timing yourself.**
   First build your skills, then work on your speed. Use the Workout as a diagnostic tool. Your score will take care of itself.

5. **Study your mistakes.**
   Look up each item you missed in the answer reviews in Appendix C. Make sure you understand why the correct answer is correct and why the wrong choices are wrong.

   Rework the problems you missed. This will reinforce what you learned from the problem; otherwise, you will be likely to have trouble with the same type of problem the next time.

6. **Classify your errors (see pages 49 and 50).**
   Classify each error as an E1, E2, or E3. Then go one step further in analyzing your E2s. Are you missing mostly algebra? Geometry? Or are you rusty on some basic arithmetic stuff?

   As you are going over your answers, keep a tally of the types of E2 errors you are making, then use that information to design your own study plan. Here are a few tips for creating a personalized math review:
   - Read the explanations for the problems in the question reviews.
   - Rework the problems you missed or were unsure of.
   - Study the Mathematics Concepts and Trigonometry Review on pages 52 through 58 of this *Study Guide*.
   - Review old math textbooks, working the chapter reviews at the end of each chapter.
   - Ask a teacher to re-explain concepts that are still fuzzy to you.
   - Form a study group.

7. **Practice.**
   Complete the entire Math Test in the ACT registration packet, available *free* in your guidance office and at **actstudent.org**.

   | Updated Score _____ |

8. **Change it up.**
   Try a different approach with the online *ZAPS* ACT-Practice Test. Find out more at www.doorwaytocollege.com/online-act-practice-test.

The Mathematics Test

9. **Keep practicing.**

    The more you work on ACT math problems, the better you will get. Practicing will do several things for you. *It will increase your familiarity with the test.* The same types of problems show up again and again on the ACT Math Test, only the situations are different. For instance, instead of having Bill buy records, they may have Sue buying books.

    The more you practice, the more prepared you will be for the types of problems you will see. *Your math skills will also improve, as well as your speed at working the actual problems.* Most importantly, *practicing will help reduce your test anxiety*, which is one of the chief causes of E1 errors.

A Word about Calculators

Don't get too excited about using your calculator on the ACT Math Test—it will not guarantee a better score or make up for the math class you slept through last year. To get a good score, you need a solid understanding of basic math concepts. You must be able to work through the math problems, not just plug a few numbers into your calculator.

The advantage of a calculator is that it may increase your speed in working through some of the problems. However, a calculator will not make up for a lack of math preparation. The best use of your calculator is to check your answers.

Begin practicing with your calculator NOW.

If you don't have a calculator, don't wait until the night before the test to go out and buy one. The calculator you take with you to the test must be one that you are thoroughly familiar with. Even the simplest calculator can have its own peculiarities. Begin practicing with your calculator *now* so that you are comfortable with it. You don't want any surprises on test day.

Don't try to use your calculator on every problem.

Many of the ACT math problems require no calculation at all, only a thorough understanding of math concepts. You can work other problems more quickly by simply thinking through the information given. If you rely on your calculator for every problem, you can end up wasting a lot of time. Practice to find out which types of problems you can solve more quickly with the aid of a calculator. First *think through* what needs to be done with the problem. What steps will you need to take? Is there a shorter way to find the answer?

Strategies

Take control away from ACT.

tip 1 Make three passes through the Math Test.

First Pass

- Go from item 1 through item 60, working only the problems you can do quickly and easily.
- Let nothing slow you down—skip any time-consuming problems.
- Aim for 100% correct on First Pass items.
- Be extremely careful—don't make careless mistakes.

Second Pass

- Go back to the beginning and start over.
- Work the harder items that you know how to work.
- Skip or guess at the demons.

Third Pass

- If you have time, try to work the most difficult problems.
- Guess at the items you can't work.
- Do not leave any blanks!

Usually, time will be running out by the end of your second pass. Don't worry about this. It is *not* critical for you to work every problem on the Math Test. It *is* critical, however, for you to check your work in order to avoid careless mistakes.

The first step of taking control of the Math Test is to shorten it up to fit your personal situation. Get real with yourself; if your starting score is around 18–20, don't fantasize about moving up to a 30. Instead, think in terms of a couple of points at a time. The number of problems you need to work and double-check depends on your target score. The following table shows what you need to do to hit various target levels.

The Mathematics Test

Reasonable Target ACT Math Score	To take control of the Math Test, you need to be . . .
30–31	correct on 54 problems, and you can blind guess on the remaining 6 problems.
28–29	correct on 50 problems, and you can blind guess on the remaining 10 problems.
25–26	correct on 40 problems, and you can blind guess on the remaining 20 problems.
21–22	correct on 30 problems, and you can blind guess on the remaining 30 problems.
18–19	correct on 20 problems, and you can blind guess on the remaining 40 problems.

For example, if your reasonable target is an ACT math score of 21, you need to use as much time as necessary to work and double check 30 of the 60 problems—even if it takes you 58 minutes. In the remaining minutes, blind guess on the other 30 problems. On average, you'll pick the right answer about six times out of 30 blind guesses. Your raw score will be about 36 and your ACT score will be about 21.

The key to making this system work is to be perfect on the number of problems that you work and double-check. Careless mistakes can ruin your ACT math score.

tip 2 Study the directions in advance.

Just as with all the ACT subtests, the directions for math items are the same on every form of the ACT.

The ACT is called a "standardized test." On every standardized test, the thing that's "standard" is the administration. This includes such variables as the length of test time, the answer sheet, the testing conditions, the level of difficulty, *and* the directions. If the directions were varied from one administration to the next, the scores would not be meaningful. In order to report valid scores, the people at ACT must be absolutely consistent in the presentation of directions. That is why you don't need to read the directions during the test—provided, of course, that you study them in advance.

tip 3 Every problem has one—and only one—correct answer.

If you know how to do the math, do it. The fastest way through these problems is usually to do the math and then find your answer among the choices. Keep a clear head as you check the format of the choices. The "best" method of solution sometimes depends on how the choices are presented.

tip 4 Do not believe any coaching that suggests you can easily find the answers by applying a series of simple tricks.

The ACT editors go to great lengths to make sure that they catch any items where tricks make a difference. As a result of their careful editing, the application of tricks is usually more difficult than the straight math.

tip 5 Check your work on every problem.

It is far more important to avoid careless mistakes than it is to race to the end of the test. There is no bonus for finishing early.

Most students check their work only if they don't find their answer among the choices. All of the problems on the ACT Math Test have predictable errors. What this means is that the common wrong answers will be included among the choices.

tip 6 Write or draw freely in your booklet (but not on your answer sheet).

You will not be allowed to use scratch paper when you take the test, so don't use scratch paper when you practice. *Get in the habit of writing all over the test booklet.* There are four purposes for this:

1. To make sketches and to compute or figure your answers;

2. To keep track of your answers, so you can backtrack if you mess up on your answer sheet;

3. To assist with your concentration on each item;

4. To help clarify the math problem that you need to solve.

tip 7 Use the Plug-'n'-*ZAP* method.

Take a look at the following problem:

45. The downtown area of Springville has parking places for 1,300 cars in three parking garages. Garage *A* will hold 200 more cars than Garage *B* and 150 less than Garage *C*. How many cars will Garage *A* hold?

   A. 600
   B. 450
   C. 400
   D. 250
   E. 200

The Mathematics Test

If you had no idea how to set up this problem, you could start by plugging in the choices and working backwards. What this means is that you *assume* one of the answers is correct and then check to see if everything fits.

Notice that the choices are placed in order from greatest to least. When plugging in choices, start with the middle one—C. If you *assume* C is the answer, does everything fit together? If it does, then C is probably correct. If C is too big or too small, you can eliminate it, and you can also eliminate two more choices based on your findings.

If we plug in **C** for Garage A . . .

Step 1:

    Garage A = **400**

    Garage B = A − 200 = **400** − 200 = 200

    Garage C = A + 150 = **400** + 150 = 550

Step 2:

    Garage A + Garage B + Garage C = 1,300

      400   +   200   +   550   = 1,150

               (this doesn't fit) 1150 ≠ 1,300

So, C must be too small. *ZAP* it. You can also *ZAP* D and E—they also will be too small.

    A. 600
    B. 450
    C̶. 400
    D̶. 250
    E̶. 200

Now you're down to a 50/50 chance. Try A. If A doesn't work, you don't have to try B— it would be the only choice left. With the Plug-'n-*ZAP* method, you only have to try out two choices, instead of all 5.

Examples of Plug-'n-*ZAP*

tip 8 — Almost every test will have problems involving averages.

Don't expect ACT to ask you a question like, "What is the average of 24, 16, and 35?" ACT average problems look more like this:

> If a salesperson sells four cars for an average cost of $10,000 each, and three of the cars sell for $8,400 each, what is the cost of the fourth car?

OR

> A total of 60 sophomores and juniors were given a history test. The 45 juniors had an average score of 85, while the 15 sophomores had an average of 90. What was the average score for all 60 students who took the test?

You need to know how to work average problems given to you in many different forms. To solve these problems, you need to identify three variables: the **Total**, **Average**, and **Number**. (Just think of getting a **TAN**.)

Usually, the ACT will give you two of these pieces and you must use the information to determine the third piece. Sometimes, you need to add a list of numbers or do some small computation to get the first two pieces before you can go after the third piece. Depending on which piece is missing, you need to use one of the forms of the following formula:

1. The Total is the Average times the Number: $T = A \cdot N$

2. The Average is the Total divided by the Number: $A = \dfrac{T}{N}$

3. The Number is the Total divided by the Average: $N = \dfrac{T}{A}$

Examples of average problems

tip 9 — Figures may NOT be drawn to scale.

This means that a side with length 8 may not be drawn exactly twice as long as a side with length 4. So, when you are given the length of one side, you cannot necessarily find the length of other sides simply by measuring. When drawings are distorted, it's usually because an accurate drawing would make the correct answer too obvious. If it's possible, make a more accurate drawing to see if you can figure out the answer more easily.

Error Types

As you prepare for the ACT, you need to pay attention to the reason behind every incorrect answer. You will probably be surprised to discover that about half of your errors are on problems you know how to solve. Under the pressure of time, it is common to make careless mistakes. After you complete each practice test, note which error type is responsible for each wrong answer.

Error 1 (E1): The careless mistake or the misunderstood question

This type of error is common for students at all levels of math ability. It occurs most frequently on the easiest items. E1 errors include things like carelessness, sloppiness, or mistakes on basic facts and simple computation. The number of your E1 errors should make you realize how important it is to be careful and check your work.

With certain types of ACT questions, you might have trouble figuring out exactly what you are supposed to do. This happens frequently with story problems. The solution is to practice over and over on your practice tests. After you finish a test once, don't feel you're done with it. If you work the same items three or four times, you will still be getting something out of your effort.

In addition to carelessness, E1 errors are often related to how intimidated you are by the ACT. If you begin the Math Test in a cold sweat, it will not be possible to think clearly and visualize every problem. The solution to this malady is practice and familiarity. By the time you have completed all of your practice tests, you should find the ACT much less intimidating. On the other hand, if you don't take the test seriously, you can also get into trouble. The idea is to be serious, but not stressed out about it.

> **For many students, E1 Errors are the most frequent type of error they make on the ACT. E1 Errors are NOT math mistakes. They are test-taking mistakes.**

Error 2 (E2): The "can't-remember-it" problem

These problems are recognizable, and you understand the question, but you can't quite recall how to do the math. For example, you might remember problems in math classes such as $(x^2)(x^3) = ?$, but you can't remember whether to add or multiply the exponents. (You add them.)

The way to minimize this type of error is to review the chapter tests in a pre-algebra, geometry or algebra math book. The review will refresh your memory and minimize E2 mistakes, and it should help reduce E1 errors as well.

> The activity of cramming for the ACT is probably worthless—in most cases. However, if you are making a lot of E2 math mistakes, a last-minute review of old math textbooks should help you reduce this type of error.

Error 3 (E3): The "never-had-it" problem

Unlike the problems that cause E2 errors, these problems require math that is completely unfamiliar to you. If your test date is scheduled in the next month or so, don't pretend that you're suddenly going to learn a whole new course in mathematics.

If you have attended a typical series of math courses, chances are good that you will see only three to five E3 situations on any one form of the ACT. If you have not been enrolled in math courses, you will need to score as many points as possible on the easier items. But don't try to cram a whole math course into one month of preparation.

Your personal error-type table

After you complete each practice Math Test, classify your errors as E1s, E2s, or E3s. Then count the number of each type of error and record it in the table below. Use the table to help focus your practice sessions.

	E1	E2	E3
Math Workout A			
Math Workout B			
Math Workout C			
Math Workout D			
Math Workout E			
Math Workout F			

The Mathematics Test

> ### The History of Story Problems
> Research indicates that story problems were created in the early 17th century by the sadistic tutor of a well-known royal family. The tutor had earlier been reprimanded for making his students sit in ground glass while performing trigometric functions. In a creative effort to avoid further punishment, the tutor invented something called *story problems* that could be inflicted on his young pupils without eliciting the sympathy of the king and queen. This method of tormenting and confusing students enjoyed immediate and popular acceptance among frustrated math teachers who had previously relied on a paddle or hickory whip to establish the proper attitude toward mathematics. . . . *Believe it, or not.*

How to Attack Story Problems

The ACT usually presents simple math in the context of word problems. The method you use to attack these problems must remain flexible because the best approach depends on the problem. Keep a clear head. Do not let yourself get muddled up. If a problem looks like it's from another planet, skip it and try the next one. In general, keeping in mind that you'll need to be flexible, you should handle story problems in six steps:

1. **Read the *question* part of the problem first.** Underline it (you'll almost always find the question in the last sentence of the story problem). This will give you a mental framework or context for the presentation of the question.

2. **Read the whole problem from the beginning.** Try to see the action or operation that is taking place. Sometimes the wording is more complicated than seems reasonable, but this is because of the need for precision in the test item. The complicated wording is less of a problem if you follow the advice in Step 1.

3. **Pull the math from the problem.** Make a sketch, write notes, or write a number sentence—anything to get you *into* the situation and to get the math *out* of the situation.

4. **Reread the problem to make sure your math works.** This procedure is one way to avoid E1 and E2 errors.

5. **Do the math.** Make sure you don't get into complex equations or computation. If you find yourself in the middle of a long, drawn-out process, you're probably working the problem incorrectly.

6. **Check your answer by plugging it into the original problem.** Even if you can't trace the math, or if you're running out of time, you must at least check your answer to make sure it's logical in the context of the problem. Also, refer back to Step 1 and make sure you have answered the question being asked.

Examples of story problems

Mathematics Concepts Review
Arithmetic and Numeration Concepts

Definitions
Whole Numbers 0, 1, 2, 3, ...
Integers ... −3, −2, −1, 0, 1, 2, 3, ...
Digits 0, 1, 2, 3, 4, 5, 6, 7, 8, 9

The Order of Operations
Use **PEMDAS** to remember the order of operations. (Mnemonic device: "**P**lease **E**xcuse **M**y **D**ear **A**unt **S**ally.")

1. **P**arentheses. Work everything inside parentheses first. Within the parentheses, follow the other rules.
2. **E**xponents. Simplify all powers and roots next.
3. **M**ultiplication and **D**ivision. Perform any multiplication and division, from left to right.
4. **A**ddition and **S**ubtraction. Perform any addition and subtraction, from left to right.

Absolute Value
The absolute value of a number is the number's distance from zero on a number line. Because absolute value is a distance, it is always a positive number. The absolute value of 0 is 0. The symbol for the absolute value of x is $|x|$.

$|5| = 5$ $|-5| = 5$ $|0| = 0$

Fractions
Addition

Fractions must have common denominators before you can add them. Find a common denominator. For each fraction, find the equivalent fraction that has the common denominator. Then add the numerators.

Example: $\frac{1}{3} + \frac{2}{5} = \frac{5}{15} + \frac{6}{15} = \frac{11}{15}$

Subtraction

Fractions must have common denominators before you can subtract them. Find a common denominator. For each fraction, find the equivalent fraction that has the common denominator. Then subtract the numerators.

Example: $\frac{3}{4} - \frac{1}{2} = \frac{3}{4} - \frac{2}{4} = \frac{1}{4}$

Multiplication

Multiply the numerators, then multiply the denominators.

Example: $\frac{3}{5} \times \frac{2}{3} = \frac{6}{15}$

Division

To divide a fraction by another fraction, multiply the first fraction by the reciprocal of the second fraction. To find the reciprocal of a fraction, switch its numerator and denominator.

Example: $\frac{1}{4} \div \frac{1}{3} = \frac{1}{4} \times \frac{3}{1} = \frac{3}{4}$

Percents
Percent means hundredths, or number out of 100.

Examples:

$\frac{30}{100} = 30\%$

2 is 25% of 8 because $\frac{2}{8} = \frac{25}{100} = 25\%$

Converting decimals to percents

Move the decimal point two places to the right and insert a percent sign.

Examples:
$0.09 = 9\%$ $0.85 = 85\%$
$0.007 = 0.7\%$ $2.13 = 213\%$

Converting a fraction $\frac{x}{y}$ to a percent

$\frac{x}{y} = \frac{z}{100}$

Example:

$\frac{2}{5} = \frac{z}{100}$

$z = 100\left(\frac{2}{5}\right)$

$z = 40\%$

Finding percent of a number

Change the percent to a decimal and multiply.

Example: What is 20% of 50?

$0.20 \times 50 = 10.00 = 10$

Ratios

Read "m is to n" and written $m{:}n$ or $\frac{m}{n}$.

Mathematics Concepts Review

Rate

A **rate** is a ratio that compares two different kinds of numbers, such as dollars per hour or miles per gallon. A unit rate has a 1 as the denominator of the ratio.

Example: Heidi read 30 pages in 2 hours. She reads at a rate of 15 pages per hour.

$30 : 2 = \frac{30}{2} = 15$

Proportions

A **proportion** is two rates that are equal to each other. Read "c is to d as s is to t." This is written as $\frac{c}{d} = \frac{s}{t}$.

You can find the missing term of a proportion by cross-multiplying.

Example:

$\frac{c}{50} = \frac{75}{250}$
$250c = 75 \times 50$
$250c = 3,750$
$c = 15$

Exponents

Positive exponents
$3^4 = 3 \times 3 \times 3 \times 3 = 81$

Negative exponents
$2^{-3} = \frac{1}{2^3} = \frac{1}{2} \times \frac{1}{2} \times \frac{1}{2} = \frac{1}{8}$

Note: $x^1 = x$ and $x^0 = 1$ when x is any number other than 0.

Multiplication/Division

To multiply exponents, if the base numbers are the same, keep the base number and add the exponents.

Example: $4^3 \times 4^2 = 4^5$

To divide, if the base numbers are the same, keep the base number and subtract the second exponent from the first.

Example: $5^7 \div 5^3 = 5^4$

When the base numbers are NOT the same, first simplify each number with an exponent, then multiply or divide.

Examples:

$4^2 \times 3^3 = 16 \times 27 = 432$
$4^2 \div 2^2 = 16 \div 4 = 4$

Addition/Subtraction

Simplify each number with an exponent before performing the operation.

Examples:

$5^2 + 3^3 = 25 + 27 = 52$
$6^2 - 2^4 = 36 - 16 = 20$

Note: If a number with an exponent is raised to another power, keep the base number and multiply the exponents.

Example: $(6^3)^4 = 6^{12}$

Algebra Concepts

Multiplying Polynomials

To multiply two binomials (an algebraic expression with two terms), use the FOIL method: **F**irst, **O**utermost, **I**nnermost, and **L**ast.

Step 1. Multiply the **F**irst terms from each binomial.

Step 2. Multiply the **O**utermost terms.

Step 3. Multiply the **I**nnermost terms.

Step 4. Multiply the **L**ast terms from each binomial.

Step 5. Simplify if necessary.

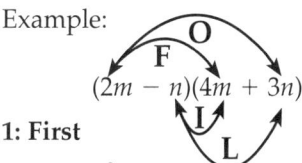

Example: $(2m - n)(4m + 3n)$

Step 1: First

$2m \bullet 4m = \mathbf{8m^2}$

Step 2: Outermost

$2m \bullet 3n = \mathbf{6mn}$

Step 3: Innermost

$-n \bullet 4m = \mathbf{-4mn}$

Step 4: Last

$-n \bullet 3n = \mathbf{-3n^2}$

Step 5: Simplify

$8m^2 + 6mn - 4mn - 3n^2 = \mathbf{8m^2 + 2mn - 3n^2}$

Solving Quadratic Equations

To solve a quadratic equation:
Step 1. Set the quadratic equal to zero.
Step 2. Factor.
Step 3. Set each factor equal to zero.
Step 4. Solve each of these equations.
Step 5. To check your work, insert each answer into the original equation.

Example:
$$x^2 + 7x = -10$$
1. $x^2 + 7x + 10 = 0$
2. $(x + 2)(x + 5) = 0$
3. $\quad x + 2 = 0 \quad$ or $\quad x + 5 = 0$
4. $\quad\quad\quad x = -2 \quad$ or $\quad\quad x = -5$
5. $(-2)^2 + 7(-2) = \quad\quad (-5)^2 + 7(-5) =$
   $\quad 4 + (-14) = -10 \quad\quad 25 + (-35) = -10$

Using the Quadratic Formula

You can use the quadratic formula to solve quadratic equations. For a quadratic equation $ax^2 + bx + c = 0$, the quadratic formula is:

$$\frac{-b \pm \sqrt{b^2 - 4ac}}{2a}$$

Example:
$$y^2 + 7y = -10$$
$$y^2 + 7y + 10 = 0$$

$$\frac{-7 \pm \sqrt{49 - 4(1)(10)}}{2(1)} = x$$

$$\frac{-7 \pm \sqrt{49 - 40}}{2} = x$$

$$\frac{-7 \pm \sqrt{9}}{2} = x$$

$$\frac{-7 \pm 3}{2} = x$$

$x = -\frac{10}{2} \quad$ or $\quad x = -\frac{4}{2}$

$x = -5 \quad$ or $\quad x = -2$

Inequalities

Treat inequalities (such as $7x + 4 > 32$) just like equations, with one exception: When multiplying or dividing both sides by a negative number, reverse the direction of the sign.

Solving Systems of Equations in Two Variables

Step 1. Choose one of the equations to work with.
Step 2. Isolate one variable in that equation.
Step 3. Substitute the value of this variable into the second equation.
Step 4. Solve for the other variable.
Step 5. Use the value of this variable to find the value of the first variable.

Example:
Solve this system of equations:
$$y + 6x = 15$$
$$4x - 3y = 21$$

Step 1. Choose one equation: $y + 6x = 15$
Step 2. Isolate one variable: $\quad y = -6x + 15$
Step 3. Substitute: $4x - 3(-6x + 15) = 21$
Step 4. Solve for x: $\quad 4x + 18x - 45 = 21$
$$22x = 66$$
$$x = 3$$
Step 5. Find the value of y: $\quad y + 6(3) = 15$
$$y + 18 = 15$$
$$y = -3$$

The solution for the system of equations is $(3, -3)$.

Solving a Function

When you solve a function, treat $f(x)$ the same way you would treat y. Solve $f(x) = 3x - 5$ the same way you would solve $y = 3x - 5$.

The Coordinate Plane

On a coordinate plane, the horizontal and vertical lines are called the coordinate axes, or the x-axis and the y-axis. The coordinate plane is divided into quadrants, labeled by Roman numerals I, II, III, and IV. The numbers in parentheses (called ordered pairs) represent points on the coordinate plane. The ordered pair $(0, 0)$ represents the origin.

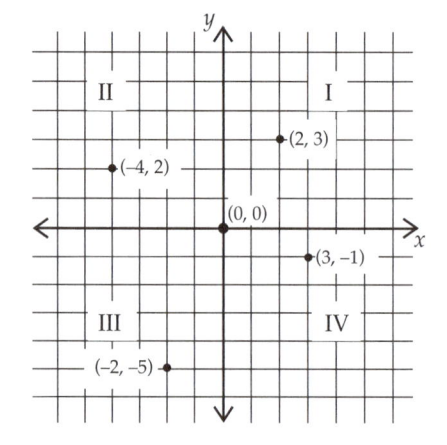

For point $(-4, 2)$, -4 is the x-coordinate and shows how far the point lies to the left or right of the origin; 2 is the y-coordinate and shows how far the point lies above or below the origin.

Mathematics Concepts Review

Slope of a Line

To find the slope of a line in a coordinate plane, use the following formula:

$$\text{slope} = \frac{\text{the difference in the } y\text{-coordinates of any two points on the line}}{\text{the difference in the } x\text{-coordinates of the same two points on the line}}$$

A simpler way to state this is:

$$\text{slope} = \frac{\text{rise}}{\text{run}} \text{ or } \frac{y_2 - y_1}{x_2 - x_1} \text{ where } (x_1, y_1) \text{ and}$$

(x_2, y_2) are points on the line.

When the slope is positive, the line goes up from left to right. When the slope is negative, the line goes down from left to right.

Graphing a Linear Equation

The graph of a linear equation is a straight line. It's easy to graph a linear equation if you get it into the form $y = mx + b$.

x and y can be any ordered pair on the line.

m is the slope of the line.

b is the y-intercept (where the line crosses the y-axis).

Example: Graph the equation $12x + 3y = 6$.

First put the equation into the proper form and simplify:

$12x + 3y = 6$
$3y = -12x + 6$
$y = -4x + 2$

The y-intercept is 2, so the line crosses the y-axis at 2. One ordered pair on the line is (0, 2).

The slope is -4. To find another point, go down 4 and right 1. To find a third point, once again go down 4 and right 1.

Draw a line through these three points.

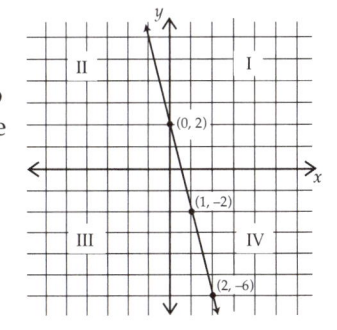

Graphing a Quadratic Equation

The graph of a quadratic equation ($y = ax^2 + bx + c$) is called a parabola. It looks like the letter U, either right side up or upside down.

x and y can be any ordered pair on the parabola. a, b, and c can have any value, except a cannot equal zero.

Geometry Concepts

Lines and Angles

Parallel lines are lines in the same plane that never intersect. Parallel lines are denoted by the symbol ||.

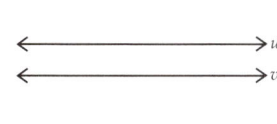

Perpendicular lines intersect to form right angles and are denoted by the symbol ⊥.

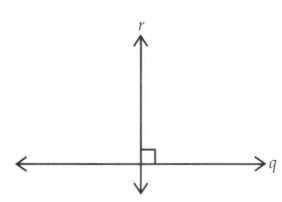

A **right angle** measures 90 degrees.

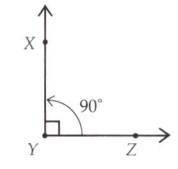

A **straight angle** measures 180 degrees.

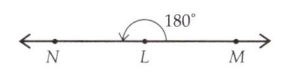

Adjacent angles share a common vertex and a common side.

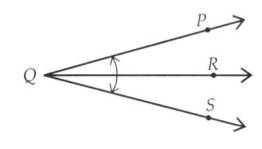

∠PQR and ∠RQS are adjacent angles.

Complementary angles are two angles whose measures have a sum of 90 degrees.

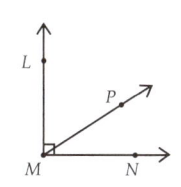

∠LMP and ∠PMN are complementary angles.

Supplementary angles are two angles whose measures have a sum of 180 degrees.

∠XYW and ∠WYZ are supplementary angles.

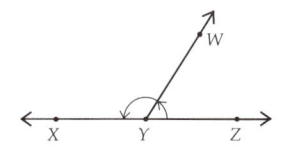

When two lines intersect, four angles are formed. The angles opposite each other are called **vertical angles** and their measures are equal. In the example below, the measures of angles 1 and 3 are equal, and the measures of angles 2 and 4 are equal.

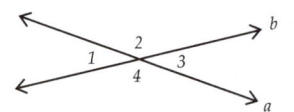

An example of **two parallel lines cut by a third line** (called a *transversal*) is shown to the right.

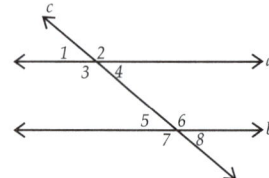

Angles 1 and 5 are called **corresponding angles** and their measures are equal.

Angles 3 and 6 are called **alternate interior angles** and their measures are equal.

Angles 2 and 7 are called **alternate exterior angles** and their measures are equal.

Similar Figures

Similar figures are the same shape but not the same size. The ratios of the lengths of corresponding sides of similar figures are equal. The measures of corresponding angles of similar figures are equal.

Example:

△ ABC and △ EFG are similar.

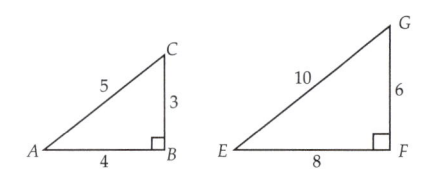

Congruent Figures

Congruent figures are the same shape and the same size. The lengths of corresponding sides of congruent figures are equal. The measures of corresponding angles of congruent figures are equal.

Example: Figure *FGHJ* and Figure *WXYZ* are congruent.

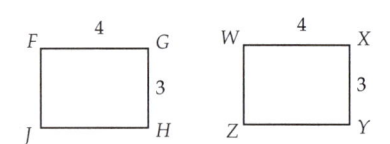

Triangles

The sum of the measures of the angles of a triangle is always 180 degrees.

The sum of the lengths of any two sides of a triangle must be greater than the length of the third side.

A triangle with all three sides the same length is called an **equilateral triangle**. Each angle of an equilateral triangle measures 60 degrees.

$$n + n + n = 180$$
$$3n = 180$$
$$n = 60$$

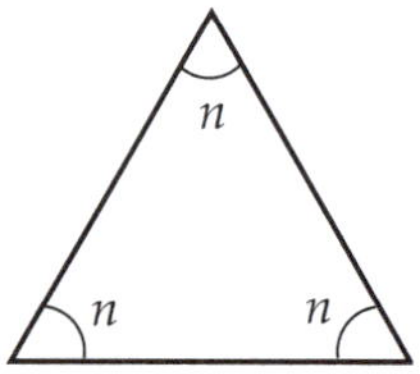

A triangle with two sides of equal length is called an **isosceles triangle**. Two of the angles in an isosceles triangle (those opposite the equal sides) are also of equal measure.

$$\angle a = \angle b$$

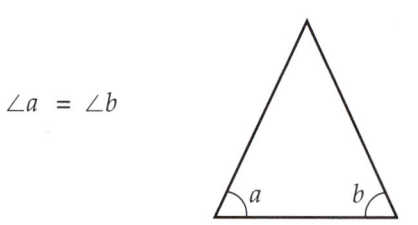

A triangle with one of its angles measuring 90 degrees is called a **right triangle**. The relationship between the lengths of the three sides of a right triangle is described by the **Pythagorean Theorem**.

The Pythagorean Theorem

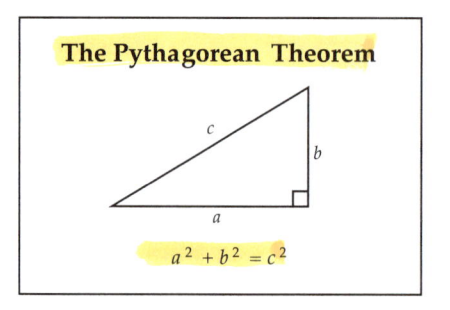

$$a^2 + b^2 = c^2$$

Example:

If $a = 6$, $b = 8$, and $c = 10$,

$$a^2 + b^2 = c^2$$
$$6^2 + 8^2 = 10^2$$
$$36 + 64 = 100$$
$$100 = 100$$

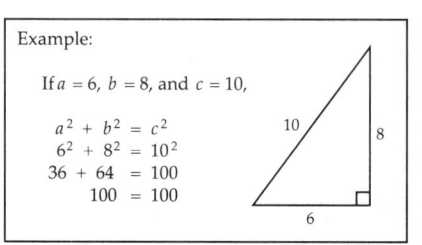

Mathematics Concepts Review

The ratio of the sides of a right triangle with angles 30°, 60°, 90° is 1:√3:2.

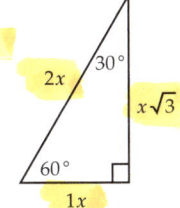

The ratio of the sides of an isosceles right triangle with angles 45°, 45°, 90° is 1:1:√2.

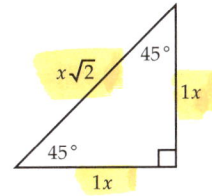

Circles

In the circle below, $\overline{AB}$ is the **radius** and $\overline{AC}$ is the **diameter**. The distance around the circle is the **circumference**.

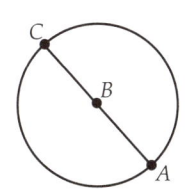

For a circle of radius r:

Circumference $= 2\pi r = \pi d$

The number of degrees of arc in a circle is 360.

Area, Perimeter, and Volume Formulas

Area of a rectangle: = length × width

Area of a triangle: = $\frac{1}{2}$ (base × altitude)

Area of a trapezoid: = $\frac{1}{2} (b_1 + b_2)$ height

For a circle with radius r: Area = πr^2

Perimeter of a rectangle = 2 (length + width)

Volume of a rectangular solid: = length × width × height

Data Analysis Concepts

Mean (the average)

To find the mean, add all the numbers in the data set and divide by the number of numbers.

Example: Aruna scores 9, 6, 12, 7, 6 on her quizzes. What is the mean of her quiz scores?

Add the scores, then divide by the number of scores.

$$\frac{9+6+12+7+6}{5} = \frac{40}{5} = 8$$

The mean (average) of Aruna's quiz scores is 8.

Median (the middle value)

Put the numbers in order from least to greatest. If there is an even number of numbers, add the middle two and divide by 2.

Example: Aruna scores 9, 6, 12, 7, 6 on her quizzes. What is the median of her quiz scores?

Put the scores in order from least to greatest.

6, 6, 7, 9, 12

The middle number is 7. Aruna's median score is 7.

If she took another quiz and scored 8, the middle two numbers would be 7 and 8. Her median score would be $\frac{7+8}{2} = 7.5$.

Mode (the most common)

In a group of numbers, the number that appears the most often is the **mode**.

Example: Aruna scores 9, 6, 12, 7, 6 on her quizzes. What is the mode of her quiz scores?

Which score did Aruna receive most often? 6. The mode of Aruna's quiz scores is 6.

A data set can have *no* mode if all the numbers appear the same number of times. It can also have *more than one mode*, if two or more numbers appear the same number of times and the most times in the data set.

Range

The range of a set of data is the difference between the largest number in the set and the smallest.

Example: Aruna scores 9, 6, 12, 7, 6 on her quizzes. What is the range of her quiz scores?

The largest number is 12. The smallest is 6.

$12 - 6 = 6$

The range of Aruna's quiz scores is 6.

Trigonometry Concepts

All of the basic *trigonometric functions* are numbers (often to several decimal places) that express the ratios of two sides in a *right* triangle for one of the two smaller *angles* (10°, 45°, 89°, 16.5°, x°, theta, etc.) in the right triangle.

The three sides of a triangle for trig purposes are:

1. the side *opposite* the angle in question

2. the side *adjacent* to the angle in question (other than the hypotenuse)

3. the *hypotenuse*, the longest side, the side opposite the 90° angle

The *sine* (or *sin*) is the numerical value that expresses the ratio of the side *opposite* the angle to the *hypotenuse*, or in trig shorthand, *opposite over hypotenuse*. It is important to remember the word *over*. In a typical example, the sine of 45°, or sin 45°, is equal to .7071.

You form a *fraction* that expresses the ratio of the two sides. Often, this is all you need to do. In a right triangle with an angle of 45°, the three sides ratio 1:1:√2. Thus the sine of 45° equals 1 *over* the square root of 2, or .7071.

Most of the work can be done using the Pythagorean Theorem ($a^2 + b^2 = c^2$) once the basic definitions are known. The SAT usually uses special triangles in test items that simplify the work, such as "3, 4, 5 triangles," "5, 12, 13 triangles," "30°, 60°, 90° triangles," etc. A basic rule of trig is: $sin(x)^2 + cos(x)^2 = 1$.

There are only SIX trig functions you need to know!

Simple Functions

First, the three *simple* functions:

1. *sin* (sine) of an angle = opposite over hypotenuse (**s = $\frac{o}{h}$, or soh**)

2. *cos* (cosine) of an angle = adjacent over hypotenuse (**c = $\frac{a}{h}$, or cah**)

3. *tan* (tangent) of an angle = opposite over adjacent (**t = $\frac{o}{a}$, or toa**)

Start by memorizing this mystical expression:

SOH, CAH, TOA

Chant this phrase fifty or a hundred times until it is burned into your brain.

Reciprocal Functions

Finally, the last three functions, the *reciprocal functions*:

These functions (*cotangent*, *secant*, *cosecant*) are reciprocals of the first three. A **reciprocal** is a fraction with its numerator and denominator reversed.

The reciprocal of $\frac{3}{4}$ is $\frac{4}{3}$.

The three reciprocal functions can also be derived by dividing various sides of right triangles by each other, but there is a simpler way to derive them. Each is just the reciprocal of one of the three simple functions:

4. *cot* (cotangent) of an angle = $\frac{1}{tan}$

5. *sec* (secant) of an angle = $\frac{1}{cos}$

6. *csc* (cosecant) of an angle = $\frac{1}{sin}$

It follows that if one of the simple functions equals $\frac{3}{5}$ or .6000, its reciprocal equals $\frac{5}{3}$.

The **reciprocal ratio** is the result, therefore, of the side that is 5 *over* the side that is 3.

Once you know the basics, you can work your way back to anything else you need to find (sides, angles, other functions, etc.) by using the Pythagorean Theorem and your knowledge of right triangles and fractions and by labeling the various sides and angles of the triangle in a drawing. Sometimes you can get the answer just by inverting a fraction, and you won't need to draw the right triangle.

All you need to remember is the information in the box below, being careful not to confuse the different functions. It would be a good idea to write them in your exam book at the first opportunity.

SOH, CAH, TOA

$cot = \frac{1}{tan}$, $sec = \frac{1}{cos}$, $csc = \frac{1}{sin}$

Radians

Radians are angle measures based on arc length in a circle with radius of 1. A 360° angle (a full circle) has 2π (pi) radians because the arc length (circumference) is $2\pi r$. So any fraction of that 360° central angle, measured in radians, will be that same fraction multiplied by 2π. For example: $60° = \frac{60}{360} \cdot 2\pi r = \frac{2\pi}{6}$ radians. Remember:

360° = 2π radians

The Reading Test

What to Expect

Four passages, 10 multiple-choice questions each. Totally ordinary. Read a passage, answer some questions. Ho hum.

The Reading Test is 35 minutes long.

Social Studies/Sciences Subscore

- One passage will cover a social studies topic.
- One passage will cover a natural sciences topic.

Arts/Literature Subscore

- One passage will present an excerpt from a literary narrative or prose fiction.
- One passage will cover an area of the arts and humanities.

At least one of the passages will be composed of two shorter selections that are related in some way. A few of the questions that follow will relate to both selections.

Total Reading Test Score

The difference between these subscores is not really meaningful. In fact, there is little validity or reliability in the subscores because a sampling of only two passages is not enough to adequately assess your ability. As far as preparation goes, your approach to each type of passage should be the same. The subscores were created to give high schools and colleges the illusion that they're getting more valuable, more detailed information.

The Reading Questions

In general, the ACT Reading Test asks two types of questions: (1) ones about details *directly stated* in the passage, and (2) ones *implied* by the passage.

More specifically, you'll be asked to do the following:

- determine main ideas
- find and interpret important details
- comprehend the sequence of events
- compare and contrast
- understand causes and effects
- determine the meanings of words, phrases, and statements in context
- generalize
- analyze the author's or narrator's voice and technique

Scoring

What does it take to achieve your personal best on the ACT Reading Test?

It's important for you to understand that the ACT is used for all students, not just others with reading ability similar to yours. A straight-A honors student receives the same test as a C or D student sitting across the room. The format and selection of passages are controlled by ACT. So what can *you* control?

==One of your biggest points of control is to decide in advance the best number of passages you will actually read. This may sound unwise at first, but some students can reach a higher personal score by attacking only two or three passages, instead of attempting all four passages.==

Let's begin with a look at the impact of ZAPPING on one passage. The ZAPPING tables below are based on a few assumptions:

1) If you read carefully and without rushing, you will "know for sure" between four and 10 answers.

2) You will blind guess or ZAP the unknown questions. (You should leave no blanks.)

3) The raw scores (number of questions answered correctly) in the tables below reflect the average results of guessing. For example, if you blind guessed on four questions with a one out of four chance, your expected gain would be two points. In actual practice, you might pick up more or fewer points. (**Note:** A *foil* is an answer choice. Each question on the ACT has four foils.)

KNOW 4 for sure	6 UNKNOWNS on one passage		
Strategy	If Blind Guess All	If ZAP 1 Foil All	If ZAP 2 Foils All
Guess Yield	1.50	2.00	3.00
Raw Gain	5.50	6.00	7.00

KNOW 5 for sure	5 UNKNOWNS on one passage		
Strategy	If Blind Guess All	If ZAP 1 Foil All	If ZAP 2 Foils All
Guess Yield	1.25	1.67	2.50
Raw Gain	6.25	6.67	7.50

KNOW 6 for sure	4 UNKNOWNS on one passage		
Strategy	If Blind Guess All	If ZAP 1 Foil All	If ZAP 2 Foils All
Guess Yield	1.00	1.33	2.00
Raw Gain	7.00	7.33	8.00

KNOW 7 for sure	3 UNKNOWNS on one passage		
Strategy	If Blind Guess All	If ZAP 1 Foil All	If ZAP 2 Foils All
Guess Yield	0.75	1.00	1.50
Raw Gain	7.75	8.00	8.50

KNOW 8 for sure	2 UNKNOWNS on one passage		
Strategy	If Blind Guess All	If ZAP 1 Foil All	If ZAP 2 Foils All
Guess Yield	0.50	0.67	1.00
Raw Gain	8.50	8.67	9.00

KNOW 9 for sure	1 UNKNOWN on one passage		
Strategy	If Blind Guess All	If ZAP 1 Foil All	If ZAP 2 Foils All
Guess Yield	0.25	0.33	0.50
Raw Gain	9.25	9.33	9.50

For purposes of illustration, let's assume that our friend Shanti knows six questions for sure and blind guesses on the other four questions. The average pickup from guessing would be one, so Shanti would gain seven points from this passage (6 + 1).

With ZAPPING, however, Shanti could pick up eight points instead of seven. When multiplied by four passages, Shanti's reading Raw Score would climb from 28 to 32. It is clear from these tables that ZAPPING increases a reading score no matter where you start on the "know-for-sure" index.

How Many Passages?

Now comes the big question: How many passages should you attack? The answer depends on your natural reading speed. Every form of the ACT will present 10 questions following each of four passages. In an effort to complete all four passages in the given time of 35 minutes, many students rush much faster than they should. Because of this rushing, they may end up gaining only four or five points per passage.

You should not move at a speed that yields fewer than seven out of 10 points. In other words, on every passage that you choose to attack, you need to answer seven to 10 questions correctly. If you can't, you need to slow down.

If our friend Shanti rushes through all four passages, the total Raw Score is between 16 and 20 points. By reading carefully, however, it should be possible for her to pick up eight to 10 points on each reading passage. The tables on the next pages show the impact of slowing down to read more carefully.

> An education isn't how much you have committed to memory, or even how much you know. It's being able to differentiate between what you know and what you don't.
> —Anatole France

Attack 2 Passages Carefully (7 of 10), Blind Guess 2 Passages	
Gain on 20 questions careful	14
Gain on 20 questions guessing	5
Raw Score	19
ACT Score*	

Attack 3 Passages Carefully (7 of 10), Blind Guess 1 Passage	
Gain on 30 questions careful	21
Gain on 10 questions guessing	2 to 3
Raw Score	23 to 24
ACT Score*	

Attack 2 Passages Carefully (8 of 10), Blind Guess 1 Passage	
Gain on 20 questions careful	16
Gain on 20 questions guessing	5
Raw Score	21
ACT Score*	

Attack 3 Passages Carefully (8 of 10), Blind Guess 1 Passage	
Gain on 30 questions careful	24
Gain on 10 questions guessing	2 to 3
Raw Score	26 to 27
ACT Score*	

Attack 2 Passages Carefully (9 of 10), Blind Guess 1 Passage	
Gain on 20 questions careful	18
Gain on 20 questions guessing	5
Raw Score	23
ACT Score*	

Attack 3 Passages Carefully (9 of 10), Blind Guess 1 Passage	
Gain on 30 questions careful	27
Gain on 10 questions guessing	2 to 3
Raw Score	29 to 30
ACT Score*	

Attack 2 Passages Carefully (10 of 10), Blind Guess 1 Passage	
Gain on 20 questions careful	20
Gain on 20 questions guessing	5
Raw Score	25
ACT Score*	

Attack 3 Passages Carefully (10 of 10), Blind Guess 1 Passage	
Gain on 30 questions careful	30
Gain on 10 questions guessing	2 to 3
Raw Score	32 to 33
ACT Score*	

*The conversion of Raw Score to ACT Score will vary slightly depending on which form of the test you happen to take. The conversion is a statistical adjustment that makes up for the unavoidable differences in the difficulty of reading passages and questions.

Practicing on Your Own

Use the following tips to work on your own and prepare for the ACT Reading Test:

1. **Do a reality check.**
   Complete one Reading Workout and determine your score using the answer key in Appendix C. As you take the test, put a star next to each question that you know for sure.

   Starting Score _____

2. **Refresh your memory.**
   Study pages 64–67 in this *Study Guide*.

3. **Continue working on the reading passages** *untimed*.
   Take as much time as you need to read one passage at a time thoroughly, and carefully work the 10 questions that follow.

4. **Check your answers.**
   Use the results to focus your practice on two areas: reasoning skills and pacing.

5. **Practice to improve reasoning skills.**
   With unlimited time, are you still missing a lot of the questions? Then focus your practice on reasoning skills.

   - Read the question reviews in Appendix C for all the items, not just the ones you missed. Go back and study the passage to make sure you understand why the correct answers are correct and why the wrong choices are wrong.

   - Study the wrong choices—why are they attractive? How are reading traps built into the test?

   - Look for questions where you could have applied the *ZAPPING* strategies.

6. **Practice to improve pacing.**
   Are you getting a majority of the questions correct with unlimited time? Then focus your practice on improving pacing. Some students will improve their score by focusing their efforts on only three passages instead of four. (But don't leave any blanks!) Others will improve their pacing by underlining and making notes as they read. Ask your English teacher or check your local library for other resources on improving reading speed.

   Remember, don't improve speed by sacrificing accuracy. It is more important to do well on the passages you have time for than it is to race to the end.

7. **Practice.**
   Complete the entire Reading Test in the ACT registration packet available *free* in your guidance office, or use the free sample tests available at **www.actstudent.org**.

   Updated Score _____

8. **Change it up.**
   Try a different approach with the online *ZAPS* ACT-Practice Test. Find out more at **www.doorwaytocollege.com/online-act-practice-test**. The Reading Test is one area where students can see a great deal of improvement with just a little bit of practice. You don't need to learn any new information; you only need to improve the skills you already possess. Go for it!

Strategies

tip 1 — Take control of the Reading Test.

During the Math Test, you took control away from the ACT by identifying the problems that were most difficult for you and either skipped them or saved them until the very end of the test. To take control of the Reading Test, the first thing you should do is skim the passages to identify the one that appears most difficult for you personally. Write "LAST" on this passage and save it for last. If you are planning to attack only three passages, go ahead and blind guess on this "LAST" passage.

tip 2 — Read the whole passage before looking at the questions.

Do not try to memorize the whole passage. Read thoroughly but quickly and then go to the questions. And don't stop reading near the end just because you're bored. Many students are anxious to get started on the questions, so they quit reading about halfway through the passage. *Bad idea!*

The exception to this tip will be the paired selections. You'll approach these in a different way, which we'll cover in Tip 11.

tip 3 — Answer all ten questions after a passage before you begin reading the next passage.

- Read all four choices.
- *ZAP* if you need to.
- Guess from the leftovers.
- Do not skip any questions. No matter how confused you are by a passage, your chances of *ZAPPING* and guessing correctly cannot possibly be better later on. Before you go to the next passage, make sure you have answered or guessed at each of the ten questions.

Again, the exception to this tip will be the paired passages, which you will approach differently. We discuss these in detail in Tip 11.

tip 4 — Underline as you read.

- Underline the first appearance of every proper noun.
- Underline expressions that keep track of sequence, such as "initial attempt" or "in earlier periods."
- Underline words or expressions that define relationships between people or ideas.

tip 5 — Make notes in the margins.

Make notes of two to three words that capture the main point of each paragraph or important idea. Together with underlining, making notes is a way to improve your control of the reading environment. This is not the place for passive reading. Read actively and assertively.

tip 6 — Circle keywords.

Certain keywords are like road signs on the highway. They tell you which way to go and warn you when the road is about to turn. If you miss these signs, you will get lost in your reading and may easily miss one or two questions. Circle them when you come to them.

Examples of Keywords

Reversal Words	Supporting Words	Result Words
on the other hand	additionally	because
however	since	so
yet	moreover	when
rather	besides	therefore
although	in fact	consequently
in spite of	furthermore	thus
nevertheless		accordingly
despite		
but		
even though		
instead		
notwithstanding		

The process of marking keywords has three major benefits:

1. It helps you focus on the reading.

2. It helps you follow the logic of the passage.

3. It reduces the amount of time you spend looking back for specific information.

tip 7 — Use outside knowledge to ZAP if you can't find the answer in the passage.

In an actual test situation, there will be times when you read the passage and then draw a complete blank on one or more items. You may also find yourself with a time problem where you have only three minutes or so to read the final passage. In these cases, even without seeing the passage, you may still ZAP many of the reading questions.

When you can't find a specific reference in a passage, don't be afraid to use your outside knowledge. It is unlikely that the answer to any question will be factually wrong. Outside knowledge could help you ZAP many of the reading items.

Even when you do read the passages, use your ZAPPING skills to eliminate choices as you first see them, so you won't waste time rereading choices that you know are wrong. As you go along, mark through the letters of the choices you ZAP.

For example, even if you did not have time to read the passage, you should be able to ZAP two or even three of the choices in the following item based on your general knowledge.

> According to the passage, the Civil Rights movement in America was LEAST active during which of the following 10-year periods?
>
> A. the 1860s
> B. the 1920s
> C. the 1940s
> D. the 1960s

tip 8 — Use True/False clues for ZAPPING.

If you are having trouble solving the problem as a multiple-choice test item, think of it as four true/false questions. Look at each choice as a true or false statement. Three statements are false—only one statement is true. If you aren't sure whether a statement is true or false, you can increase your odds of getting the correct answer by using giveaway words to tip the scale.

Check for words that would give away one or two of the choices as false statements. Giveaway words will help you evaluate whether a statement is more likely to be true or false.

Examples of Absolute Words (usually indicate false statements)	Examples of Ambiguous Words (more likely to appear in true statements)
all	some
always	often
every	may
must	seem
no	most
never	usually
none	many

The Reading Test

The following item presents an opportunity to ZAP on the basis of giveaway words. This strategy should be applied only in situations where you don't have time to read the passage or where you have already read the passage but it didn't make any sense to you.

> Which of the following most accurately states the artist's position as implied by the first sentence of the passage?
> A. Every piece of art is equally worthy of praise.
> B. Art is an activity that supersedes most others.
> C. All innovative art is attractive to the general public.
> D. Art and society usually influence each other.

tip 9   When time is running out, look for questions that provide line or paragraph references.

These questions can usually be answered without reading any more than a small portion of the passage.

tip 10   Study the wrong choices offered on the Reading Test in order to become aware of how the ACT editors are trying to trap you.

The editors at ACT *do not* expect you to be illiterate—they *do* expect you to be careless. They build traps to catch you in your careless reading habits.

If you study the wrong choices for the reading items, you will begin to understand how they are trying to trap you. And you will learn how to avoid the traps.

tip 11   Take the paired selections one at a time.

At least one of the passages on the Reading Test will be a set of shorter, paired selections that are somehow related. Following these selections, you'll see a few questions for each selection, then a few related to both selections. Here's how you should approach these passage sets.

Step 1: Read the first passage, then jump to the questions related to that passage and answer them.

Step 2: Go back and read the second passage, then answer the questions related to it.

Step 3: Answer the questions related to both passages.

By reading the passages and answering the questions in this order, you'll be less likely to get confused and more likely to get the greatest number of questions correct.

> Science is a way of thinking much more than it is a body of knowledge.
> —Carl Sagan

The Science Test

What to Expect

Ordinary is definitely *not* the word for the Science Test. The ACT editorial staff designed and developed the Science Test to assess your *reasoning* ability, not so much your knowledge of science. In actual practice, it's a test of technical reading comprehension based in scientific situations. In your science classes, you probably have been exposed to the basic concepts as well as the types of charts, tables, graphs, and diagrams on the test.

The science you need is presented within the test itself. If it weren't for the time limit, this would probably be the favorite test for many students. It's more like a puzzle than any of the other subtests, and it could be a lot of fun for students who like a real challenge.

The test is only 35 minutes long. In that time, you'll need to study and understand three passage types:

- Research Summaries (45–55%)
- Data Representation (30–40%)
- Conflicting Viewpoints (15–20%)

After gaining a thorough understanding of each information set, you'll need to answer a few questions. In general, the quickest questions to answer correctly will be the charts and graphs questions found in the Data Representation passages.

Scoring

What does it take to achieve your personal best on the ACT Science Test?

Your two main points of control on the Science Test are: 1) your selection of which passage type to attack first; and 2) your allocation of time to each passage type.

==Most students find the Charts & Graphs passages easier than the others.== If you spend 33 out of 35 minutes just on Charts & Graphs, your science score could still hit the national average, as illustrated below:

Use most time on CHARTS & GRAPHS Blind Guess Other 25 Questions	
Gain of 14/15 on Charts & Graphs	14
Gain of guessing on other 25 questions	6 to 7
Raw Score	20 to 21
ACT Score	

Use most time on CHARTS & GRAPHS ZAP Other 25 Questions	
Gain of 14/15 on Charts & Graphs	14
Gain of ZAPPING other 25 questions	8 to 13
Raw Score	22 to 27
ACT Score	

If you find after practice that you prefer the Experiments passages, you could hit the national average by spending nearly your entire time just on these three passages, as illustrated below:

Use most time on EXPERIMENTS Blind Guess Other 22 Questions	
Gain of 16/18 on Experiments	16
Gain of guessing on other 22 questions	5 to 6
Raw Score	21 to 22
ACT Score	

Use most time on EXPERIMENTS ZAP Other 22 Questions	
Gain of 16/18 on Experiments	16
Gain of ZAPPING other 22 questions	7 to 11
Raw Score	23 to 27
ACT Score	

Regardless of which type of passage you attack first, allow as much time as you need to have confidence in every answer. Even if you require 25 minutes to carefully attack the first three passages, your total score will be higher than if you carelessly rush through the entire test.

The Science Test

The tables below represent reasonable strategies for students of various ability levels. It is not unusual even for straight-A students to run out of time on the ACT Science Test. ==The most important control issue here is for you to define your strategy in advance, and then stick to it when you take the test.==

Strategy for Straight-A Student Attacking Entire Test at Manageable Pace	
Gain 14 to 15 Charts & Graphs	14 to 15
Gain 15 to 18 Experiments	15 to 18
Gain 5 to 7 Reading	5 to 7
Raw Score	34 to 40
ACT Score*	

Strategy for B+ Student Attacking Test at Strategic Pace	
Gain 14 to 15 Charts & Graphs	14 to 15
Gain 13 to 15 Experiments	13 to 15
Gain 2 to 3 Reading	2 to 3
Raw Score	29 to 33
ACT Score*	

Strategy for B Student Attacking Test at Strategic Pace	
Gain 13 to 14 Charts & Graphs	13 to 14
Gain 12 to 14 Experiments	12 to 14
Gain 2 to 3 Reading	2 to 3
Raw Score	27 to 31
ACT Score*	

Strategy for B/C Student Attacking Test at Strategic Pace	
Gain 13 to 14 Charts & Graphs	13 to 14
Gain 9 to 11 Experiments	9 to 11
Gain 2 to 3 Reading	2 to 3
Raw Score	24 to 28
ACT Score*	

*The conversion of Raw Score to ACT Score will vary slightly depending on which form of the test you happen to take. The conversion is a statistical adjustment that makes up for the unavoidable differences in the difficulty of the science passages and questions.

Practicing on Your Own

Use the following tips to prepare for the ACT Science Test:

1. **Do a reality check.**
   Complete one Science Workout and determine your score using the answer key in Appendix C. As you take the test, put a star next to each question that you know for sure.

   Starting Score _____

2. **Refresh your memory.**
   Study pages 73–78 in this *Study Guide*.

3. **Continue working only one information set (passage) at a time.**
   You don't need to complete an entire Workout at every sitting. You'll get sick of it and never want to look at the ACT again. It's better to do a little bit every day over a long period than to bulldoze ahead and then quit in frustration.

4. **Don't worry about your score or about timing yourself.**
   First, build your skills, then work on your speed. Become familiar with the test format, the types of information sets presented, and the language and style in which the passages are written. Focus on improving your skill at efficiently and effectively reading the graphs, charts, and tables.

5. **Pay attention to the wrong choices, even on problems you got correct.**
   Just like the Reading Test, there will be traps on the Science Test. What is it about the wrong choices that makes them attractive to you? Examining the wrong choices will help you begin to understand how test editors think and what types of traps they set for unsuspecting students.

6. **Study your mistakes.**
   Look up each item you missed in the answer explanations in Appendix C. Why is the correct answer correct? Why are the wrong choices wrong? Are you missing more questions on one particular type of information set than on the others?

7. **Practice.**
   Complete the entire Science Test in the ACT registration packet available free in your guidance office or at **actstudent.org**.

   Updated Score _____

8. **Keep practicing.**
   One of the best ways to improve on the Science Test is to become more familiar with scientific writing. In the long run, you could do this by reading magazines like *Scientific American*. In the short run, just practice reading and working the ACT science passages. The more familiar you are with the actual test style, the better you will be at attacking the information sets. With a little practice, they can actually be fun!

9. **Change it up.**
   Try a different approach with the online *ZAPS* ACT-Practice Test. Find out more at **www.doorwaytocollege.com/online-act-practice-test**.

The Science Test

Strategies

tip 1 — Take control of the Science Test.

Just as with math and reading, you need to take control of the Science Test. This is easy to do if you know your strengths and weaknesses. For example, decide while practicing which type of science passage is easiest for you. If you don't know which passage type will help you pick up the most points, the test editors will determine which passage type you do first, next, and last. Why not choose the order that works best for *you*?

tip 2 — Study the test format in advance.

Before the day of the test, study the three passage formats to see how they are similar and different. Notice the kinds of questions that accompany each passage type. Although your own ACT test will have different topics and subject matter, the format and types of items will be the same as these. The more familiar you are, the more quickly you will be able to move through this test. This is an opportunity to gain a serious competitive advantage over students who are unprepared for the Science Test.

tip 3 — Pick up the easy points first, then work through the harder items.

Quickly identify each passage type: Data Representation, Research Summaries, or Conflicting Viewpoints. Write letters to indicate the passage type (DR, RS, or CV) at the top of the page. The Data Representation passages only have questions about graphical information. Sometimes there may be charts and graphs within a Research Summary passage, but Research Summary passage sets will ask other types of questions as well.

First: Start your work with the information sets containing Charts & Graphs. Doing the Charts & Graphs passages first is generally the best way to pick up points in a hurry.

Second: If you are a good reader, attack the Conflicting Viewpoints passage next. If you are not a good reader, tackle the Research Summaries; these contain charts, graphs, or tables, so they may offer some relatively quick points compared to Conflicting Viewpoints. But be careful; don't spend too much time trying to understand the finer details of an experiment if you're not comfortable with science. Answer the questions you're sure of, *ZAP* what you can, guess from the remainder, and go on.

Third: Attack the remaining passage type. Which passage type you save for last is up to you, just be sure you never, never leave any blanks.

tip 4 — Notice the small details.

Pay close attention to any text information presented in the passage. Read the title of each graph and table. Study the labels on both the horizontal and vertical axes of every graph. Study the tables and diagrams that accompany the experimental summaries. Study the labeling and function of any components presented in a schematic diagram.

tip 5 — Compare the information across data sets.

You can expect to be asked a lot of questions about more than one data set at time within a science passage. Think about how the data sets relate to each other. Make written notes comparing the information as you try to answer the questions.

tip 6 — Understand the two types of questions for Charts & Graphs questions.

There are two general types of Charts & Graphs questions.

Data questions ask you to:
- Identify values
- Compare values

With *trends and relationships questions*, you may be asked to:
- Identify the shape of a graph
- Determine the relationship between values
- Extrapolate (extend) graph lines to identify trends

tip 7 — Don't confuse rate and time.

Be careful when working problems that involve rate and time. ACT will ask questions that concern the time (duration) of an experiment, as well as the rate (speed) of the reaction. Be sure you understand the difference between time and rate.

The Science Test

tip 8 — Choose the correct units — and convert your answer if necessary.

Take the time to make certain you're choosing the right units. And if you come up with millimeters, but the answer choices are all in centimeters, be sure you do the conversion correctly to get the right answer.

tip 9 — Use the reading tips on the science passages.

Remember, the Science Test is really a test of technical reading. The tips for the ACT Reading Test (pages 64 through 67) will also work on the science passages. Mark up the passages with underlining, circling, and notes.

tip 10 — Determine each author's viewpoint(s).

For Conflicting Viewpoints passages, quickly determine where each writer stands on the topic discussed. Is one writer completely *pro* and the other one *con*? They might disagree strongly, or they might have minor differences of opinion. They may even agree with each other on minor points. Note how each writer feels by using + and – signs. This will help you to quickly spot areas of agreement and disagreement.

tip 11 — Make friends with the Scientific Method.

You don't have to be a scientist to do well on the Experiments passages, but it will help to be on a first-name basis with the Scientific Method. Understanding the Scientific Method will help you understand an experimenter's point of view, how an experiment is set up (the *variables*, *control*, and the experimenter's *hypothesis*, for example), and whether the results support the researcher's hypothesis and/or conclusion.

By understanding the Scientific Method, you'll be prepared to answer questions like these: "Do the results of the experiment support the researcher's statement that …?" "Which of these steps should the researcher have taken if the substance had been flammable?" "Based on Hypothesis A, which of the following graphs shows an expected result?" "Which hypothesis is *weakened* by the results shown in Table 1?" "Which assumption must you make to understand the results of the experiment?"

tip 12 — You won't be tested on scientific terminology.

The ACT will not test you on the meaning of words like *endothelium* or *bacillus* or *magnetometer*. And you won't be expected to know the vocabulary of physics, biology, earth science, astronomy, or chemistry, either. So relax when you see scientific or technical terms, and just think logically to answer the question.

tip 13 — Every question has one—and only one—correct answer.

If it sometimes seems to you that two answers are correct, first double-check the question, then go back to the information set. If two choices still appear to be equal, then they are probably both wrong, since they cannot both be correct. Although the ACT editors are not infallible, the odds of you catching them with two correct answers are about zero in a million.

tip 14 — Use only the information given in the passage—not experiments you did in class.

The girl sitting next to you may be a physics star who has done enough force and motion experiments to win the Nobel Prize. But if she relies on her own experience to answer the ACT questions, she might still get them wrong. The point here is to use only the data that's in front of you. Don't think you can outsmart the test editors by pulling in the results from an experiment you did in class or a video you watched on the Internet. Use only the information given, because that's the information you're being tested on.

tip 15 — Trust your intuition, but verify if necessary.

In items where all four choices need to be considered, quickly ZAP any choice that seems intuitively wrong. Then examine the remaining choices. If you are unable to verify that one of these is the answer, go back and reconsider the choice that you instantly ZAPPED; it's possible that you ZAPPED the correct answer by accident.

tip 16 — Don't make easy questions hard.

Since you need to do so many items, some of them will be fairly easy. Look at Question 9 on page 35 of Science Workout F (go ahead and turn to the problem in your Science Workout booklet; we'll wait for you):

> Based on the information obtained from the experiments, which of the following would have been a likely net change in the length of the zinc rod used in Experiment 1 if its length had been 25 cm?

Looking quickly at the table, we see that the zinc rod in Experiment 1 was 100 cm, and it expanded to .175 cm. A rod only 25 cm would be 1/4 as long as the 100 cm rod used in the experiment. So, the 25-cm rod would expand 1/4 of .175. All we need to do is divide .175 by 4 to get the answer.

The Science Test

tip 17 Watch out for the negativity trap.

Many questions contain a negative twist, such as:

- Which of these contradicts X?
- Which of the experiments does NOT support Z?
- Which of the following discoveries would weaken the theory of Scientist Q?
- To which of the following would the data be LEAST relevant?
- Which of these was NOT a critical factor in the experiment?

Although the word *not* is typically given in all caps in the ACT, other negative words may not be highlighted at all. Take a minute to identify and circle the negative words in the questions above. Questions like these must be handled carefully—and with deep concentration. It's very easy to get turned around as you consider all of the choices. When that happens, you might reach a correct conclusion, but answer the item incorrectly.

When you're taking the Science Test, circle any negative terms and make sure you keep them in mind as you read the choices. Then make a notation by each choice, such as *yes/no* or *y/n* or +/− or even *pro/con*, or whatever makes sense to you. These simple notes will minimize the possibility of confusion and could save you two or three important points on the test.

tip 18 Keep moving.

You need to work at a very healthy pace to finish on time. Although you should study the passages with some intensity, don't dawdle on any of the items. If you stop and really contemplate every choice, you'll have difficulty completing the test.

tip 19 At the five-minute warning, adjust your strategy.

When you hear the five-minute warning, take a quick assessment of where you are. If you're on the last page, you may be able to work through to the end without concern. But if you have a lot of questions left to answer, it's time to switch into a different gear. Use that time to take a shot at ZAPPING through the remaining items. If you can ZAP one choice out of each of the last 12 items, you should pick up four or five points even though you may not have been able to read the final two or three passages. Do not leave any blanks, but do make a note in the margin to show where you stopped working and started guessing.

When you get to the end, return to where you left off and continue working. As you determine each correct answer, simply erase the previous incorrect guess. Don't let time run out while you still have three or four blank spots on your answer sheet. On the ACT Science Test, every question is worth nearly a point.

Attacking ACT Science Graphs

On the ACT Science Test, you won't have time to thoroughly study each chart or graph. With only 60–90 seconds to spend on each information set, it will be important for you to use your time wisely. Below are four simple steps to maximize the use of your time. Quickly do the first four steps, and you'll have a much better chance of finding the correct answer to the question.

STEP 1: Identify the main idea—the title.

When you see a graph on the Science Test, the first thing you should do is find out what it's about. Most graphs will have some sort of title. In some cases, you will need to read a paragraph to find out the subject of the graph.

STEP 2: Identify the variables.

- What is the horizontal variable?
- What is the vertical variable?
- Is there a third variable? Sometimes there will be. Many students miss one of the questions because they overlook a third variable.

STEP 3: Identify the scales.

- Are the scales continuous or categorical?
- What are the units of measure?
- What are the minimum and maximum values on the scales?

STEP 4: Read the question.

ACT Science Test questions generally fall into one of two categories:
- Questions asking you to read or determine a value.
- Questions asking you to understand trends and relationships.
- Know what you're being asked before looking for the answer.

> Aerodynamically, the bumblebee shouldn't be able to fly. But the bumblebee doesn't know it, so it goes on flying anyway.
> —Mary Kay Ash

Appendix A

Seminar Pages

Guessing—Case Study #1

The ACT English Test includes 75 items. What if you knew 55 answers and blindly guessed on the other 20 items? Tough Test #1 shows that, on the average, students will gain five raw score points from blind guessing on 20 items.

Case Study #1 ACT ENGLISH TEST SCORE		
	RAW SCORE	**ACT SCORE**
Without Guessing	55	
With Blind Guessing	60	

No matter how poorly you guess, any difference will always be in the positive direction. You can't hurt your score by guessing.

When you're guessing, do so quickly. A fast guess is just as good as a slow guess.

Appendix A

Tough Test

This "Tough Test" is based on the 20 hardest questions ever to appear on the ACT. These questions represent situations where most students need to guess.

Before you guess at each answer, wait for full directions from your instructor.

TOUGH TEST #2

#				
1	(A)	~~B~~	~~C~~	D
(2)	~~F~~	G	(H)	~~J~~
3	A	~~B~~	(C)	~~D~~
4	~~F~~	~~G~~	H	(J)
(5)	A	(B)	~~C~~	~~D~~
6	~~F~~	(G)	H	~~J~~
7	(A)	~~B~~	~~C~~	~~D~~
8	F	(G)	~~H~~	~~J~~
9	~~A~~	~~B~~	C	(D)
10	F	(G)	~~H~~	~~J~~
(11)	~~A~~	~~B~~	C	(D)
(12)	F	(G)	~~H~~	~~J~~
13	(A)	~~B~~	~~C~~	D
(14)	~~F~~	G	(H)	J
15	~~A~~	(B)	~~C~~	~~D~~
16	~~F~~	~~G~~	~~H~~	(J)
(17)	A	~~B~~	C	~~D~~
(18)	~~F~~	(G)	~~H~~	J
(19)	A	~~B~~	(C)	~~D~~
(20)	(F)	~~G~~	~~H~~	J

The Effects of Smart Guessing on the ACT

Write the number you got correct in the box below.

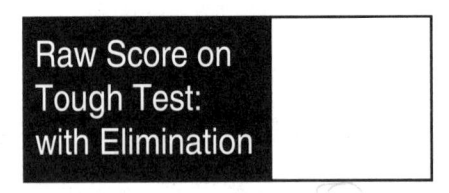

Raw Score on Tough Test: with Elimination	

If we gave this Tough Test to a million students, the average score would be 11. If your score was higher or lower than 11, it was simply by chance.

This Tough Test clearly demonstrates that not all guessing is alike. The only difference between blind guessing and the Tough Test is that some of the choices were eliminated on the Tough Test. This helped you zero-in on the right answer.

On the real ACT, you can often eliminate two or even three choices.

Guessing—Case Study #2

Just like Case Study #1, let's say you knew 55 answers on the ACT English Test. You again had to guess on the other 20 items. This time, instead of blind guessing, you were able to eliminate some of the choices before guessing.

In other words, you zeroed-in on the answers and then picked from the leftovers. You were guessing on both tests—but on the Tough Test you were guessing between fewer choices. The average gain on the Tough Test is 11 extra points from zeroing-in before guessing.

Case Study #2
The Effects on Guessing on the ACT Test

	RAW SCORE	ACT SCORE
Without Guessing	55	21
With Blind Guessing	60	23
With Eliminating Choices		

What a difference!

If you eliminate choices before you guess, you increase your odds of getting the correct answer—and your score will go up!

Appendix B

Score Conversion Tables

Estimated ACT Scores Based on Practice Test Results

Note: The tables used by ACT are slightly different for each form of the test.

Estimated ACT Score	Number Correct on English Test	Number Correct on Math Test	Number Correct on Reading Test	Number Correct on Science Test	Estimated ACT Score
36	75	60	40	40	36
35	—	—	39	39	35
34	74	59	38	38	34
33	—	58	37	37	33
32	73	57	36	36	32
31	72	56	34–35	35	31
30	71	54–55	33	34	30
29	70	52–53	32	33	29
28	69	49–51	31	32	28
27	68	47–48	30	31	27
26	66–67	44–46	29	29–30	26
25	64–65	42–43	28	28	25
24	62–63	39–41	27	26–27	24
23	59–61	37–38	26	25	23
22	57–58	35–36	25	23–24	22
21	54–56	32–34	24	22	21
20	51–53	30–31	22–23	20–21	20
19	49–50	27–29	21	19	19
18	46–48	25–26	20	17–18	18
17	43–45	22–24	19	16	17
16	40–42	20–21	18	14–15	16
15	37–39	16–19	17	13	15
14	31–36	13–15	15–16	11–12	14
13	29–30	Blind 12 Guessing	13–14	Blind 10 Guessing	13
12	26–28		12		12
11	20–25		11		11
10	Blind 19 Guessing		Blind 10 Guessing		10
9					9
8					8
7					7
6					6
5					5
4					4
3					3
2					2
1					1

Scores 36–33: 99th Percentile*

Scores 22–21: National Average

*Percentile rank is based on ACT scores of high school graduates from 2010, 2011, and 2012.

Appendix B

Estimating Your ACT Score

Step 1: Record your estimated ACT scores for one of each Workout. Add your estimated ACT scores in the box labeled "Sum of Scores." (Choose your higher English score.)

Test	Workout ACT Score
English	~~12~~ ~~15~~ ~~25~~ 15 / 19
Math	15
Reading	
Science	
Sum of Scores	

Step 2: Use the tables below to find your estimated total ACT score.

Sum of Scores	Estimated Overall Score	Sum of Scores	Estimated Overall Score	Sum of Scores	Estimated Overall Scores
142–144	36	106–109	27	70–73	18
138–141	35	102–105	26	66–69	17
134–137	34	98–101	25	62–65	16
130–133	33	94–97	24	58–61	15
126–129	32	90–93	23	54–57	14
122–125	31	86–89	22	50–53	13
118–121	30	82–85	21	46–49	12
114–117	29	78–81	20	42–45	11
110–113	28	74–77	19	38–41	10

> If a man empties his purse into his head, no man can ever take it away from him. An investment in knowledge always pays the best interest.
> —Benjamin Franklin

Appendix C

Answer Reviews

English Workouts 88

Mathematics Workouts 108

Reading Workouts 139

Science Workouts 151

English Answer Review
Workout A

1-D D is the only choice that is not redundant, since the words "must have" and "certainly" mean the same thing in this context. Always look for such redundancies, since they often appear on the ACT.

2-H H is correct because a gerund is called for. A gerund is a verb form that ends with "ing" and functions as a noun. The first use of the word "running," in "upright running" is in the gerund form. The second use must use the gerund form to remain parallel. F is wrong because the infinitive form "to run" is not parallel. G and J are wrong because both "it" and "the same" would seem to refer to "upright running" instead of just "running"—implying that upright running is possible on four legs.

3-B This sentence is presented in the present tense. "Upright running is . . . and the physical structure and musculature it requires make . . ." ZAP A, C, and D because these choices use the past tense, "required." Note that the plural verb "make" is required to agree with the nouns "structure and musculature." These are two separate things. If you're confused about the correct verb, substitute "they" for the two nouns: "They make", not "They makes."

4-J The sentence only makes sense if the pronoun "it" refers to the development of bipedal locomotion. Since this is unclear, good style demands that a noun such as "the change" be used in order to indicate the meaning clearly.

5-B A retains the original sentence fragment. B creates a grammatically correct sentence. C creates a new sentence fragment. D is wrong because a sentence fragment cannot be joined to a sentence with a semicolon.

6-J F and G can be ZAPPED because no punctuation is required between the words "fours" and "and." The coordinating conjunction "and" is sufficient to link the parallel words "run" and "pick up." The word "both" requires that "and" be used instead of "to," so H can be ZAPPED. You must get item 5 correct to answer this correctly.

7-B A is a run-on sentence. The subordinating conjunction "although" (D) is wrong because the two parts of the sentence it connects complement each other and should be linked with "and."

8-G The playful tone and nonscientific observations make it clear that the author has a humorous intent in this part of the passage (G). It is important to identify the style and tone of passages as you read them. Expect to find a fairly wide range of narrative styles on the ACT. G is also correct because the sentence connects the first person who used a stick to challenge a tiger with another person who successfully defended his cave with a sharpened stick. F is incorrect because the idea of tigers being deadly adversaries is not essential to the discussion; the adversary could just as well have been a snake or a mastodon. H is incorrect because the passage discusses how early humans improved their ability to fight off tigers by improving their weapons. J is wrong because this is not an academic discussion and because the sentence adds value both by reinforcing the tone and by illustrating the lack of success of early humans in fighting off predators.

9-D Whether to set off the clause with dashes or parentheses is an editorial choice, as long as you remain consistent. Choice D uses parentheses, which is okay, but throws in unnecessary commas.

10-J Which choice best describes the underlined portion? Choice J. Choice F does not match the content of the underlined part at all. The sentence is still talking about events in the past, not today (G). The sentence is about more than just gathering food (H).

English Answer Review Workout A

11-D The phrase, "the methods *used to bring art* to the eyes," is clear, concise, and grammatically correct. Choices A (the form that appears in the passage), B, and C are awkward and too wordy. Phrases such as "is able to be" instead of "can be" are often reason enough to ZAP a choice. A, B, and C represent a type of wrong answer that appears often on the ACT English Test. This option is usually longer than other choices and uses more words than are necessary to express the intended idea. Often these phrases don't sound like something people would really say. Trust your ear. If something sounds pompous or stilted to you, and the rest of the writing in the passage does not, there is a good chance that you are right and that the option should be ZAPPED. Here's a trap you should watch for: Don't read the passage and simply choose an answer that will make the phrase in the passage work a little bit better. B improves A in this way, but both are still wrong. Be prepared to throw out the sound of the underlined portion of the passage and go with a different-sounding version entirely, one that attacks the problem of expressing the intended idea from a different direction. The best strategy is to ZAP all of the obviously wrong choices, then substitute the remaining ones for the underlined part of the passage. With practice, you will learn how ACT English questions work and the right steps to take for each item. Knowing these steps intuitively means that you can apply them fast enough to get your best score.

12-F F is correct because no punctuation is needed between "press" and "to" in the sentence, despite its length. Compare it to a sentence such as: "We have to work to succeed." Grammatically speaking, they are the same. It is often helpful on questions like this to make up a shortened version of a sentence with the same structure in order to simplify the problem.

13-C Although possessive nouns use an apostrophe followed by an *s* (Frank's hat, the team's victory, the town's center), this is not the case with the pronoun *it*. The *'s* form of this pronoun is used only for the contracted form of "it is," as in "It's a beautiful day." The correct form for the possessive of *it* is "its." This rule, like many rules of English grammar and usage, is not strictly logical. It is a rule that must be memorized. Several questions involving the use of an apostrophe and *s* with "it" are certain to be on the ACT.

14-F Choice F offers the best transition between the general discussion of technological impact in Paragraph 1 and the specifics found in Paragraph 2. F also serves as an effective topic sentence for Paragraph 2. H is an example of the technological change discussed in Paragraph 2, but it would be a better fit later in the paragraph. G and J are details that don't fit.

15-C Questions such as this ask you to use your judgment to make a change in the passage. C is the best choice since it is the only one that would not add a comical or illogical image to the passage. Learn to recognize the writing style and tone that are being used in a passage. No correct choice will ever depart very far from the overall tone of the passage. Chances are good that if a choice seems a little "strange" to you, it is wrong and should be ZAPPED.

16-F "World" is a singular noun. It needs to be possessive because the "museums" are "of the world," just as in "Frank's hat," the hat is "of Frank." In the possessive form of singular nouns and pronouns (with the exception of "its"), the apostrophe goes before the *s*. In plural nouns, the apostrophe follows the *s*. For example, "When the aliens returned to their worlds, they put the objects in their *worlds'* museums."

17-D A can be ZAPPED for two reasons. First, some punctuation is needed after "treasures" to indicate that it completes an independent clause (an independent clause has all the parts of a complete sentence and could stand alone as a sentence). Second, no comma is needed between "now" and "a computer." B and C can be ZAPPED because *both* a comma and a word such as "and" or "but" are needed to separate two independent clauses. The rule that applies is: "Independent clauses may be separated by a comma *and* a coordinating conjunction such as *and, but, for, or, yet,* etc." D is correct because it separates the sentence into two complete sentences.

18-G F is wrong because the passage contains an obvious sentence fragment: "That are displayed anywhere in the world." H is wrong because a semicolon does not belong between "paintings" and "that." A semicolon cannot be used to join a fragment to a sentence. In almost all situations on the ACT, a semicolon is only used to join related independent clauses (clauses that have all of the parts of a sentence, express a complete thought, and could stand alone). The choice here is between a dash (J) and no punctuation at all (G). The dash is wrong because the phrase "paintings that are displayed anywhere in the world" describes what the "images," not "the paintings," are "of." Using the dash would change the intended meaning and suggest that the computer "images" are displayed throughout the world. Note that while this final choice is a difficult one to make, your chance of getting a correct answer is greatly increased by first ZAPPING F and H.

19-A The two verb forms must agree. Since the passage is correct as it stands, your ear should not detect anything wrong with it, and you should go on to examine the other three choices. B is wrong because "will look" places the looking action in the future. The action described by the verb "see" is taking place in the present, at the same time as the actions of "enlarge" and "restore." The verb "had used" places the artist in the past. C does take place in the present, but the word "if" makes the painter's action conditional. Therefore, the "would" form is necessary in order to make the painting's present appearance conditional as well. In the same way, D takes place in the past but is not conditional. Try reading the sentence with the different choices to see that it only works as it appears in the passage. Notice that "would look"—a choice that is not given—would also have worked, although it would have changed the sentence's meaning slightly.

20-H This one should be easy if you learn to recognize a run-on sentence. A run-on sentence is two complete sentences (or two independent clauses) combined into a single sentence. The type shown in the passage (F) is a "fused" run-on sentence, meaning that no punctuation is used. G is a comma splice; a run-on sentence that uses a comma to join the two sentences. J is not exactly a run-on sentence, since it uses the conjunction "and" to join the two sentences. J is wrong, however, for two reasons. The first is that these sentences should not be joined by a conjunction, since they are not that closely related. The second is that even if the two independent clauses were closely related, joining them with a conjunction would require the use of a comma after "works." H separates the two sentences properly by placing a period after "works" and capitalizing the word "The."

21-A The word "Art" is singular, as is the word "it." B can be ZAPPED for the same reason. The choice is between A and C. The ACT will often ask you to choose between a comma and a dash in situations like this. The comma (A) is correct here because the phrase "rather than gazing mutely at it," is initially set off from the sentence by a comma. Therefore, a comma must appear at the end for balance. If a dash preceded "rather," C would be correct.

22-H This question requires you to choose the correct form for the verb "filter." By eliminating intervening words we can see that filter is part of the verb phrase "by adjusting and . . ." Only H works in the phrase, because, like "adjusting," it uses the "ing" ending.

English Answer Review Workout A

23-B A would keep a comma-spliced run-on sentence in the passage. C attempts to fix the problem, but a careful reading of the new sentence shows that it really makes no sense. Between B and D, the choice is B, because the word "while" correctly suggests that the two trends are merely occurring at the same time, whereas the word "since" incorrectly suggests that the first causes the second.

24-F H is wrong because it would create a comma-spliced run-on sentence and because the pronoun "it," which is singular, refers to "recording techniques," which is plural. G creates a pronoun problem. J has the correct pronoun, but creates a comma-spliced run-on sentence.

25-A The question asks which sentence would effectively develop the meaning of the previous sentence. The previous sentence, after being shortened by question 24, dealt with the ability of recording techniques to alter the sound of musical performances. A develops this idea by suggesting that the improved techniques can actually create a second performance that can be thought of as just as "real" as the original. B raises the new subject of compact disc players, something that was not mentioned in the passage. C states that new possibilities for recording "fidelity" have occurred. This may be true, but the previous sentence dealt with the alteration of original sounds, not their faithful preservation. D might work if the sentence contained some proof that the recording techniques discussed were evident to a casual shopper. Since it does not, the sentence does little to develop the previous sentence and raises new questions which it does not answer.

26-G This question requires that you use your ear to eliminate sentences that are awkward or contain errors. F is awkward because the word "first" is located in an odd position. Did Schnitger tap his cane somewhere else later? Did other people tap their canes later? Did Schnitger tap on the floor with something other than his cane later? Also, the sentence implies that Schnitger used only one technique, cane-tapping, to plan the organ. G, on the other hand, makes a simple statement which tells what Schnitger did and how the activity was related to organ-planning. G should be left un-*ZAPPED* and the next two choices should be read to see if they work. H is constructed oddly and uses more commas than it ought to. H also doesn't tell us where Schnitger tapped his cane nor how that is related to planning an organ. J is no better than H. Notice how it uses "first" next to "planning." Of course you plan first. You don't need to say both.

27-C The details of Paragraph 3 support the central idea of Paragraph 4. References to ''a large cathedral'' and ''an intimate night club'' are examples of changing the ''character of the sounds.'' Paragraph 3 should, therefore, follow Paragraph 4.

28-J If you read the passage carefully, you should realize that the author deliberately avoids expressing an opinion. This should allow you to *ZAP* F and G, the two "yes" choices. H can be *ZAPPED* because the passage does mention various kinds of art. The correct "no" answer is J, because the task described could have been easily completed without discussing the various kinds of electronic art, but the failure to express any opinion at all on the central issue clearly falls short of the assignment.

29-B No punctuation is necessary after "humans."

30-G Since an idea very similar to this one has already been clearly stated in the expression "Almost since the beginning of time," the entire phrase is unnecessary.

31-C The main idea of the first paragraph is the wide range of useful products produced for and by humans from bulrushes. C gives an actual example of a famous bulrush product and would be interesting to most readers. It is the choice that best fits the criteria given in the question. Vivid examples are often the best choices for questions such as these.

32-F A colon is needed to link the statement to the words "sewage treatment." The statement implies that it will be directly followed by the name or names of the thing that it is discussing, a situation that requires a colon. None of the other forms of punctuation, or lack of punctuation, would work here.

33-A B, C, and D are all awkward for a number of reasons. The word "discovered" is preferable to the longer form "made the discovery" even without the various complications that this usage creates in the other three choices. A is the shortest and simplest choice.

34-J "Containing" is shorter and more direct than "in which there are" (G). F is clearly awkward. H uses the phrase "polluted by . . . pollutants," which is redundant.

35-D The word "currently" means "right now" and calls for the present tense, so A and B can be ZAPPED. C can be ZAPPED since commas are not necessary to set off an adverb placed between a verb form such as "are trying."

36-H Breaking this long, complicated, and grammatically flawed sentence into two parts is clearly the best choice in terms of style. When a choice on the ACT is two shortened sentences that retain the intended meaning and are grammatically correct, it is usually the best choice.

37-C While the passage does conclude with hopeful words about the future uses of bulrushes to combat pollution (A), it does not contain persuasive language that attempts to influence readers to take action (C). The passage mentions how bulrushes purify water but does not provide scientific detail (B). Although it mentions scientists (D), the passage contains general information about the history and uses of bulrushes over time, not just about how scientists employ them.

English Answer Review
Workout B

1-B The words "widely" and "by many" both modify the verb "believed" and communicate the same idea. When both are used the sentence is redundant. B is the only choice that eliminates one of the words.

2-F F correctly uses the verb "to declare". There is no reason for the comma in B, and the words "to be," "as," and "is" are all unnecessary and examples of poor diction. When the shortest answer to an ACT English item seems correct, it is usually the best choice.

3-D One "nation" is being spoken of, so the singular form of the possessive is called for.

4-J The rule of parallelism applies here. The nouns in the series "law," "commerce," and "government" call for a fourth singular noun to be used to complete the sentence.

5-C The simplest choice is the best. All of the others are unnecessarily complicated.

6-F G and H are too wordy and introduce unnecessary clauses into the sentence. J is wrong because the meaning is made somewhat unclear by separating "call" and "for independence." F is another example of "shorter is better."

7-C A pair of commas is needed to set off the explanatory phrase "where the local dialect is essentially a separate language" from the main clause. C and B are the only choices that include the first of these two commas. B is wrong because the phrase "which is" is unnecessary.

8-F The first part of the paragraph deals with distrust and resentments that have arisen from language differences. To reinforce this theme the sentence would have to give further evidence of this phenomenon. F is the only choice that does this.

9-A "Bring about" is the only one of the four choices that means "cause." It is clear from the rest of the sentence that this is the intended meaning.

10-H Two contradictory ideas are suggested by this portion of the passage, and a word such as "however" is needed to show the proper relationship between them.

11-D The subject of "suggests" is "examination," which is a singular noun. C and D are the only choices that give the correct form of the verb. C is wrong because no comma is necessary.

12-J J states the intended meaning of the sentence in the clearest form. Each of the other sentences has problems with usage, sentence structure, and word choice.

13-B The original passage contains a sentence fragment. It is an introductory clause and should be separated from the sentence that follows it by inserting a comma.

14-H The subject of the sentence should be a plural pronoun referring to the words "immigrant groups." "Their" is the only correct choice for such a pronoun.

15-C C is the best choice from a stylistic viewpoint. It is the only option that is not awkward and wordy. It states the intended idea completely and fully. Read each of the other choices to yourself and notice the ways in which they are awkward and unclear. With practice, you should be able to ZAP each of them quickly and go on to the next question without spending much time.

16-G The point made by the previous sentence concerns the enrichment of the English language by the addition of foreign words and phrases. F and G both deal with the subject of foreign languages being brought to America, but G is better because it gives actual examples of the phenomenon. H and J introduce new subjects rather than reinforce the earlier sentence's point.

17-B The passage as it stands contains a comma-spliced run-on sentence. Two complete sentences convey the clearest expression of the intended meaning, as in B. C and D attempt to eliminate the run-on sentence by creating subordinate clauses, but the meaning of the sentence is unclear in both cases.

18-F Placing the sentence at Point A offers an additional reason why some people believe English should be declared America's official language, so it's a good fit with the main idea of the paragraph. If placed at Point B, the sentence would directly contradict the sentence it would follow. The middle section of Paragraph 2 discusses the ways in which new immigrants soon adopt English. The last part of Paragraph 2 would contradict the sentence if it were placed at either Point C or Point D.

19-D The underlined portion is unclear. North Carolina and Nashville are far-flung and distant from what? A change is desirable. Deleting the word *two* (Choice B) doesn't make the statement any clearer. The word *either* takes a singular noun, so Choice C can't be correct. The sentence is grammatically correct and accurate without the underlined portion.

20-J F is wrong because a comma is needed to set off the introductory phrase from the main clause. G is wrong because the present tense is used to describe an event in the past. H, however, uses the correct tense, and the choice is between H and J. J, which creates an introductory phrase separated by a comma, is shorter, less awkward, and conforms to standard usage.

21-B No comma is necessary between "planters" and the phrase describing the planters, so A and D are wrong. The word "who" is used correctly, while "such as were" is a wordy example of nonstandard usage. Once again, the shortest gramatically correct expression is the best one.

22-J "Emigrate from" and "leave" refer to the same noun and have the same meaning, so only one is needed. *ZAP* F, G, and H. The only choice that eliminates this redundancy is J.

23-D This item requires you to take into account the comma after Ulster. You're not free to eliminate this comma. Therefore, B and C would ruin the sentence. *ZAP* them. Your choice is between A and D. A is awkward. *ZAP* it.

24-H F is wrong because it is unclear who "they" are. G and J are awkward. J is the shortest and clearest answer.

25-B The previous sentence states that the Scots in Ulster were isolated from other groups. A description of this isolation (B) would be the best way to strengthen this point.

26-G As used here, the words "intolerable" and "unbearable" have the same meaning. Their function is to suggest that the Scots wanted to leave Ulster, and either word would be sufficient for this purpose. G is the only choice that eliminates the redundancy.

27-C Choice A leaves a sentence fragment in the passage. B is wrong because a comma is necessary to separate the main clause from the adverbial clause. As you read the sentence, you can hear a natural pause after "left." C uses the comma correctly. D incorrectly uses a semicolon. A semicolon will not work where a period won't work.

28-J F is wrong because the paragraph at this point is primarily about the heavy Scottish migration to Philadelphia, not the English settlers who were already there. G also develops the wrong idea, Philadelphia's development, as does H. J is the best choice since it provides interesting modern-day evidence of the Scottish migration during the period discussed.

29-C A is a comma-spliced run-on sentence. B looks all right, but it is no better than D. Both can't be right, so B and D can be *ZAPPED*. C is a correctly punctuated compound sentence. No comma is necessary in D, and the word "therefore" is unnecessary since the idea is clearly implied by the rest of the sentence.

English Answer Review Workout B

30-H No punctuation is required between "dialect" and "sustained." All of the other choices create sentence fragments and are clearly wrong.

31-A A states the idea simply and is punctuated correctly. The commas used to set off "and the oral tradition" are wrong in B. C uses a plural verb form ("lives") where a singular form ("live") should be used. D is a tempting choice, but it is not as good as A because it uses extra words and punctuation for no apparent reason.

32-G You should learn the meanings of the easily confused "their," "they're," and "there." "Their" is the possessive form of "they," so G and J are the only possible correct choices. The extra words "those who are" in J are unnecessary, making G correct.

33-D A singular possessive form is called for. D is the only choice that has the proper ending.

34-F F is the shortest and best answer. G uses "like" with a verb form where "as" should be used. H introduces the noun "it" without a verb to accompany it. J gives "it" the passive verb form "is believed to be," but the expression is awkward and confusing compared to F.

35-A Choice A is a simple and clear way to state the intended idea. B and C use the pronoun "you," but it is not clear who "you" refers to. D is awkward and wordy.

36-H No comma is called for, so G and J can be ZAPPED. A careful reading of the sentence indicates that the action took place in the past, so the form "would have been" should be used instead of "will have been."

37-A No comma is needed between "ballads" and "sung." The past participial phrase "sung in the Scottish lowlands in the days of James I" acts as an adjective, modifying the noun "ballads." The formation is no different grammatically than the expression "bicycle built for two." Therefore, B and D can be ZAPPED. The past participle of "sing" is sung. Therefore, A is the correct choice.

38-G Paragraph 2 mentions the frontier life of the Scots-Irish; therefore, it is the best place to discuss their reputations as pioneers. Paragraph 1 is mostly about their origins in Europe and paragraph 3 is about their modern descendants. A new paragraph at the end would disrupt the chronology of the passage.

English Answer Review
Workout C

1-B Subject-verb agreement. The subject "distinctions" is plural, so the verb "was" needs to change to "were"; ZAP C. No commas are needed, so both C and D can be ZAPPED.

2-F Parallel verb forms. "Building shelter" is a task, along with "gathering food" and "making clothing," so the verbs "gathering," "building," and "making" are parallel; all should be in the same form and are correct here.

3-D "Usually in most cases" is redundant. D is the only answer that corrects this redundancy. Adding punctuation (B and C) doesn't fix the redundancy. This is a common trap. When you spot unnecessary punctuation in an answer choice, ZAP it.

4-F No change. Although the underlined portion seems long, none of the answers improve on this, and each introduces a punctuation error.

5-C A sentence fragment precedes the period. Although the fragment is disguised as a long group of words, your clue is the word "with" at the beginning of the sentence. If you can't use a period, you can't use a semicolon.

6-H Faulty parallel. The words "creation" and "correcting" carry equal weight in the sentence and should be parallel in form and case. Since both belong to "problem," they must have the singular possessive case: "problem's creation" and "its correction."

7-D Shorter is usually better, and in this case, you should delete the whole portion. The words "which should be avoided whenever possible" are obvious and therefore add nothing new about the ideas of "greed for profits," "prevalent disease," "widespread suffering," and "poverty."

8-H Subject-verb agreement. The subject "culture," which follows the verb "were," is singular; therefore, "were" should change to its singular form, "was." A colon (G and J) may be used to introduce a list, but there's no list here.

9-C Shorter is usually better. Choices A, B, and D all add unnecessary words.

10-G Punctuating a nonrestrictive phrase. The phrase "with their nimble fingers and small size" is a nonrestrictive modifier that should be set off with commas. (A nonrestrictive modifier is not vital to the meaning of a sentence.) Looking ahead of the underlined portion, you should have noticed a comma. A single comma will never come between a subject ("children") and its verb (were), so a second comma is necessary between "children" and "with." Adding a dash after children would work if the comma after "size" were also a dash. Dashes work in pairs; you can't use one dash and one comma to set off a nonrestrictive clause.

11-B A sentence fragment follows the underlined period, so A (NO CHANGE) can be ZAPPED. C can also be ZAPPED because a semicolon, like a period, only connects complete sentences. (If a period won't work, neither will a semicolon.) B and D both correct the fragment, but D is longer than necessary.

12-J "Bad" and "inadequate" are redundant. Only J corrects this redundancy.

13-D Awkward writing. Two phrases in a row are introduced with "which," making the sentence sound clumsy. B creates a sentence fragment. C removes a comma instead of correcting the real problem. D simplifies the sentence and removes the comma, directly connecting the "spread" to "epidemics."

English Answer Review Workout C

14-G Subject-verb agreement. The pronoun "some" can take a plural or singular verb, depending on what it refers to. Here, it is plural, referring to some of the factory owners. (Compare "Some of this banana is bruised" to "Some of these bananas are bruised.")

15-B Shorter is better. Although the phrase, "where the problem usually tended to be greater than it was in agricultural countries," seems to say a lot, it doesn't add any new information and therefore should be deleted.

16-J Whole-passage question. You must read each choice and decide if it is true or false. F states that the writer's opinion is so strong that the writer may be disregarding fact or reason in favor of his or her opinion. If so, a reader won't know what to believe. This is not true, for the issue of child labor is well known, and the author's opinion isn't unique. ZAP F. Also, since this issue is well known, it would be easy to find facts to support the passage. ZAP G. H says that opinions should never be stated in an essay without support. There can be exceptions to this. When a choice on the ACT uses words like "never," "always," and "everybody," there is a good chance that choice is wrong. ZAP H. J is a gentle critique, calling for just a few specific details. J is reasonable.

17-A Whole-passage question. The passage gives general information about child labor practices. It doesn't argue against these practices, as though it were persuading people against child labor (B). It is too general for a college course (C), and it has little to offer for someone trying to protect children today (D).

18-F "Its" is a possessive pronoun for "America" and is correct as used here. Do not confuse "its" with "it's," which is a contraction of "it is."

19-A Verb tense. The verb form "could grow" is consistent with the tense of the paragraph. See the following verbs from the first three lines; your ear should tell you that they go together: first line, "*has* held"; second line, "*could* grow"; third line, "*have* faced."

20-F Previous-sentence box question. F is a concrete example of what the first sentence says. As a general rule, try to support a statement with undisputed facts. The first sentence here says that America has promised that anyone could grow up to be whatever he or she wanted. The second sentence states a common belief that the presidency is not beyond anyone's reach (F)—an indisputable example of what is meant in the first sentence. G says what is already said in the second sentence. H is unrelated. J is too general.

21-C Antecedent-pronoun agreement. When a pronoun is underlined, check for its antecedent. The antecedent for "it" is "advantages of education or geographical mobility." This antecedent requires that you use the plural pronoun, "them," and that it be correctly punctuated within a nonrestrictive modifier. A nonrestrictive modifier can be separated from the sentence by a pair of commas or a pair of dashes, but not a combination of both.

22-G Shorter is usually better. The word "in" is not needed in the underlined portion. "Their" and "there" are homonyms with very different meanings; be sure you know which is which.

23-B Previous-sentence box question. The previous sentence says our parents and grandparents usually accepted the jobs that came their way. To demonstrate the reality of this, the writer should cite concrete examples. B gives the reader examples: "farm," "market," "dock," and "factory work."

24-H A fragment follows the period. Since question 25 does not correct the fragment, it depends upon question 24 to do so. G is wrong; if a period doesn't work, neither will a semicolon. J is wrong; the colon won't work because the next sentence is not an example of what is stated before the colon.

25-C Antecedent-pronoun agreement. The pronoun refers to "parents" and "grandparents" three lines earlier. "Their" is the correct plural possessive pronoun.

26-J The comma splits the predicate and should be removed. This sentence is similar to "I'm glad that you are here." A comma wouldn't work after the verb "glad."

27-A No change. Choices B and D invite you to incorrectly change the tense of the verb. C and D tempt you by introducing a semicolon, which would create a sentence fragment.

28-G Previous-sentence box question. Expanding an idea is easily accomplished by citing concrete examples. "Vocational counselors," "job fairs," "books on career changing" are examples that elaborate on the previous sentence's mention of "endless number of careers."

29-D Run-on sentence, or a comma splice. A comma incorrectly used to connect two clauses. Since the two sentences must be properly separated, you can ZAP A and B. Although *yet* can be used to connect two sentences, it does not correctly describe the relationship between the two clauses. "Yet" implies contrast. D is correct because the colon demonstrates that the words "when we are free to choose . . . circumstances" are an example of "the blessing is clear." Note that this must be solved with question 30.

30-G The comma between "choose" and "our life's work" makes the sentence more clear. Otherwise, a reader may think that the author means to say "when we are free to choose our life's work," instead of "when we are free to choose, our life's work does not have to be. . ." The semicolon will not work because the first clause is not complete (H). J is a workable choice, but since it achieves the same effect as G, the word "then" is unnecessary.

31-A Diction. This question is inviting you to replace "for example" with a different phrase. This isn't necessary because the surrounding sentence is an example, or clarification, of the "darker side" mentioned in the previous sentence. It does not set up a contrast; ZAP C and D.

32-J Whole-paragraph question. It is important to view all of the choices before choosing an answer. Only J suggests not beginning a new paragraph, while G and H are really no better than F. The phrase "the result being" is probably the result of something said in the previous paragraph, and should be included in that paragraph. Note also that "the result being" is an awkward construction, so you'd immediately want to ZAP A.

33-D You'll run into many situations like this when you take the ACT. The writing is simply not very good. About all you can do is ZAP both A and B, and then decide whether leaving out "providing" is better than inserting it. What you're looking for here is a phrase that is parallel with "personal and professional satisfaction." Try adding "as well as a hefty income" to the list: "a source of personal and professional satisfaction—as well as a hefty income." The answer is D.

34-H Run-on sentence. H is the only choice that separates the two sentences.

35-A Paragraph 3 presents an idea that contrasts with the central point of Paragraph 2. Paragraph 4 draws a conclusion regarding the contrast. Paragraph 3 should therefore remain where it is.

English Answer Review
Workout D

1-D   A sentence fragment follows the period. A and B will leave a fragment. C and D will correct the fragment, but only D will preserve the parallel structure. "Result of pure chance" is grammatically parallel to "lucky event" and must be placed in a parallel position within the sentence. Your ear should tell you that C is incorrect.

2-F   No change. A long introductory phrase is usually set off by a comma. As you read the sentence, you should feel a natural pause after "story."

3-C   Verb form. The author is using the passive voice: "Fleming was presented." The passive voice tells the reader what has happened ("presented with the miracle of penicillin") and to whom ("Fleming"). Fleming wasn't doing the presenting; rather he was being presented with something.

4-F   Possessive case. For most nouns, the singular possessive is formed by adding an *'s*. A possessive noun does not have to be a person's name.

5-C   Whole-passage question. As a general rule, essays present an idea and support it with examples. Often, one paragraph states an idea and supports it with examples called *supporting sentences*. Explaining the discovery of penicillin will take several paragraphs. This is acceptable because the main idea is still being supported by examples.

6-F   Punctuating nonrestrictive modifiers. The words "a man who . . . years" is an appositional statement that modifies "Fleming." Since this kind of modifier restates what was said previously, it is a nonrestrictive modifier and should be set off with commas — or one comma, if it is at the end of the sentence.

7-A   Concreteness. The previous sentence alludes to background information about Fleming. A sentence about his scientific interests as a student would be a logical addition to the background information.

8-G   Parallel structure. A comma is not needed between items with parallel status within a clause. "Isolating" and "identifying" are parallel. This is like the sentence *Apples and oranges are my favorite fruits*. You wouldn't put a comma after *apples* or *oranges*.

9-A   Punctuating nonrestrictive modifiers. This must be solved with 10; in fact, it may be easier to do 10 first. With the underlined words of 10 removed, this phrase is an appositional statement that modifies "battle." Since this modifier is vital to the sentence, it should be separated with a comma and not made into its own sentence (C and D).

10-J   Shorter is usually better. The comment about World War I adds no useful information to the sentence.

11-D   Shorter is usually better. "Possessed of the capability" means the same thing as "was able to."

12-G   Whole-passage question. The passage's main point is to get the reader to reconsider the story of penicillin's discovery: not that it was pure luck, as is often believed, but a result of Fleming's skill, insight, and good fortune. An audience of science teachers would already know this (F). If the audience were ignorant of Fleming (H), the author wouldn't have to dispel the myth. There is no point presenting an argument to scientists who already know it (J); such a group would want to hear something new.

13-B Whole-passage question. The quotation referred to is an example of what the author meant when he or she said that Fleming's discovery was luck or pure chance. As a rule, examples should follow general statements.

14-G The sentence contains two verbs: "concerns" and "has led." One of them has to be removed. Changing "concerns" to "concerning" makes the phrase "concerning the existence of life under very hostile conditions" a modifier of "discovery."

15-D Redundancy. "Wonder" and "ask themselves" are redundant. Only D eliminates the redundancy.

16-J Shorter is better. The phrase "quite like any other known microbe" doesn't need to be introduced with "which is" (F) or "that is" (G). H changes the meaning of the sentence by suggesting the bacteria that was recently found lived a long time ago. Another clue that the sentence is flawed is in the comma following "Bacteria." There should be two commas or none. Since you can not insert another comma after "microbe," J solves the problem by allowing you to remove the comma.

17-B Sentence fragment. A sentence fragment follows the period, so A and C won't work (a semicolon cannot replace a period). B is correct because a comma is not needed after "found." The sentence is similar to "I found my keys by looking under the table." You would not need a comma after "keys."

18-H Subject-verb agreement. The subject is "water temperature," and the correct verb is "was recorded." Answer J tempts you with a shorter option, but careful reading will show that you cannot omit the verb.

19-C When possible, sentences should be followed with examples that capture the reader's interest. A, B, and D are things a textbook would list. Since this is an essay, it needs to be more interesting than a textbook. C has a gory appeal that may interest a reader; in addition, it develops the idea in the previous sentence.

20-J F and H prompt you to make a punctuation error. G introduces a subtle inaccuracy: the bacteria do not thrive "without needing" the benefit of light; they thrive "without the benefit" of light. In addition, "there" reminds the reader that the bacteria are from the deep ocean.

21-D Verb form. The verb "have gave" is incorrect. Removing "have" corrects the grammar without changing the sentence. B and C create redundancies ("earlier" is redundant with "previous" and "once").

22-F The complete idea is "thought to be drawn." This is the way the sentence should be written. To omit the words "to be" (J) leaves the sentence a little vague. Shorter is only better when no meaning is lost.

23-A Phrases beginning with "which" are frequently separated by a comma. "That" and "which" often can be used interchangeably, which is your clue that B and C are unacceptable. If you chose B or C, you would be saying that the black smoke bacteria leaks sulphurous gases. D would create a sentence fragment.

24-J The sentence is redundant with the previous sentence. Notice that the previous sentence says, "Scientists are looking with interest for answers to some of life's mysteries . . ." Every other choice is awkward.

25-C The first sentence of the passage mentions the "possibility of life on other planets." It is appropriate for an essay to return to an idea that was referred to in the beginning.

26-J Shorter is usually better. Only J gets to the point without loss of detail.

27-B The reader does not know who "they" refers to, so you can ZAP A. C is too long. D changes the meaning of the sentence by implying that the gland's powers are called "the master gland." B eliminates the problem by restating the phrase in passive voice—"it is called."

English Answer Review Workout D

28-H The sentence following the period is a fragment, and so is the solution offered in J. G would create a run-on sentence. H correctly connects the fragment to the previous sentence.

29-A No change. If you omit the words between the subject and the verb, you will see that the subject is "one," which doesn't correspond to the verbs "were" (B) or "are" (D). C changes present tense to past tense, which is unnecessary.

30-H F and J invite you to incorrectly use the possessive case. The possessive of "it" is "its," not to be confused with "it's" (it is). G invites you to use long and cumbersome language.

31-B The phrase "which is an abnormal state" is redundant. We know that gigantism is an abnormal state, so the phrase is unnecessary.

32-F This passage is a formal essay of the type that might appear in a textbook. Compare the tone of a formal essay with the tone of a letter from a friend. The letter might have phrases such as "wouldn't you know," but a formal essay would not. "But wouldn't you know" is too informal.

33-C The underlined words have two problems: 1) they create a run-on sentence, and 2) they are redundant. The comma should be eliminated, as should the extra verb (*was*). The phrase "the most" is redundant with "smallest." C corrects the run-on sentence and removes "most."

34-J The sentence says three things were made by the finest craftsmen: clothing, shoes, and furniture. A list of three items should be punctuated as shown in this explanation. Since these three items are a subject for the verb "made," you would not put a comma after "furniture."

35-A The words "such as arthritis" are an example of "uncomfortable symptoms." This type of modifier is set off with commas. Choices B and C create sentence fragments.

36-H The essay is addressing hormone disorders, and only H makes it clear that the disorders that are becoming less common are growth-hormone disorders.

37-B Shorter is better. Any technique that humans use to produce a growth hormone will be a synthetic technique. In using the shorter version (B) you also remove a redundancy.

38-F The phrase "While this enables doctors to help prevent dwarfism" is correctly punctuated. This question is trying to get you to introduce a punctuation error.

39-D The singular verb needs to be plural. "Pituitary glands and growth rates" is the compound subject for the verb "is." The correct form should be "are." B will not work because "remains" is also in the singular form. C changes the meaning.

40-J An essay should focus on one topic and stay on the subject. Although the discussion of dwarfism is appropriate, the paragraph about the two famous dwarfs is largely unrelated to the topic of disorders and treatments related to the growth hormone.

English Answer Review
Workout E

1-D Punctuation. The phrase, "about two of the ocean's better known inhabitants" is crucial to the meaning of "confusion." Without the phrase, the reader would not know what the confusion is, so this phrase should not be separated from the word "confusion" by a comma. The semicolon in B creates a sentence fragment. C separates "deal" from "confusion," which is no better than the original.

2-F Verb tense. Since the paragraph is in the present tense, the present tense form, "represent," is appropriate.

3-C The underlined portion creates a fragment by separating the phrase from its sentence. B creates a fragment, because a semicolon can only join two complete clauses. D uses the word "including" twice, making the sentence awkward.

4-H Whole-paragraph question. The first two sentences prompt the reader to wonder what the difference between dolphins and porpoises is. The third sentence gives an answer based on their scientific classification.

5-D The phrase "their family name is *Phocaenidae*" is a nonrestrictive modifier. Such a modifier must be set off with dashes or commas. Either could be used, and a choice between these would be unfair, but D is the only one that uses the same punctuation before and after the clause.

6-J Shorter is usually better. The commentary "which is . . . weighed" is unnecessary and should be deleted. Choice G creates a sentence fragment; H misuses commas, as the original does.

7-C A and B would each create a sentence fragment. D would separate "that dazzles us" from "creature," the noun it modifies. Because the noun most closely preceding the pronoun "These" or "This" is singular ("bottle-nosed dolphin"), we need a singular pronoun. In this case, the correct pronoun is "This" (B and C). B would create a sentence fragment. The correct answer is C.

8-G A sentence fragment follows the period after "whale," and, in this case, the fragment adds no worthwhile information. The sentence is better with it left out.

9-B Diction. C and D make the sentence longer than necessary. The difference between A and B is in the choice of preposition, "on" or "of." "Of" sounds better.

10-H Diction. Neither "answer," "issue," nor "problem" makes sense in the sentence. "Distinction" does because it implies something you would use to separate the two species. Note that the word "difference" is in the following line.

11-B Subject-verb agreement. The subject is "difference," although it is easy to assume that "two" is the subject. "Difference" is singular, requiring "is" instead of "are."

12-F Whole-passage question. The passage implies that it is going to tell us how to tell the two species apart, but then fails to do so. This is the weakness of the passage, which could be corrected by some explanation of the distinction between the two species.

13-A Correct as is. The question is tempting you to change the punctuation when no change is necessary.

14-F This is a good place to use ZAPPING. ZAP H because it's too wordy. ZAP J because you don't capitalize the word following a semicolon. The only difference between F and G is the insertion of the word "is." It's unnecessary. Remember, when you get down to two choices, and they both look good to you, shorter is better. ZAP G.

English Answer Review Workout E

15-C Sentence fragment. A sentence fragment follows the period. Since "homes" and "historic sites" are parallel, they should be joined by "and" rather than with a comma.

16-J Diction. This sentence contrasts a "desirable place to live and work" and the "richest and most interesting places in America for a family vacation." The words "not only" best prepare the reader for this contrast.

17-C Pronouns. The correct form of the reflexive pronoun is "themselves." This sentence is similar to "I can help myself." You would not say, "I can help me."

18-J Shorter is usually better, and, in this case, it is the only phrase that will not sound clumsy.

19-D Shorter is usually better. The comparison to Los Angeles is unnecessary and should be omitted.

20-F "Early" and "original" are redundant.

21-D Diction. Since more than two sites are alluded to ("Betsy Ross's house," "Christ Church," "Independence Hall," and the "Liberty Bell"), "best" should be used instead of "better," which reduces the choices to C and D. D offers the shortest version.

22-H Sentence fragment. A fragment follows the period. A colon won't connect the two parts because "Near the Delaware River and its docks" is not an example of the "east side of town" (G). A semicolon won't work because it can only join complete clauses (J).

23-A Possessive pronouns. "Its" is the correct possessive pronoun for "Delaware River" and should not be confused with "it's," which means "it is."

24-G Punctuating nonrestrictive modifiers. This problem should be solved with 25. The phrase, "a time when European sailing ships were loaded there with agricultural and forest products" is appositional and should be set off with commas.

25-D "From upriver" is part of the appositional phrase "a time when European sailing ships were loaded there with agricultural and forest products," which modifies "three hundred years ago." It should not be separated from the rest of the phrase.

26-H The first thing to decide in this type of question is which paragraph should come first. Obviously not #3, so ZAP J. Which paragraph seems more "introductory," #2 or #1? This is a close call, but #2 is better. ZAP F. Now the choice is whether #3 or #1 should come next. At the end of #1, the writer calls Center City "one of the most interesting places for a family vacation" and says, "visitors have … theme park." This leads to a list of places "visitors … are in a city and not a theme park." #1 should follow #2, and #3 should be last.

27-A Whole-paragraph question. Paragraph 3 deals with Philadelphia's history (A), not architecture (B), Penn's design (C), or the muddy river bank (D).

28-G The second and third sentences need to be connected, otherwise they make no sense. How could it be a "certainty" that railroads could make a town rich when the owners often "changed their minds" or "went bankrupt"? The word "but" should be used to set up this contrast. H and J do not.

29-A The current possessive form is correct. The merchants are "of the town." You could say "town merchants" (D), but you would have to keep the comma. D removes the comma.

30-H If you omit the portion between the dashes, the sentence reads, "The town's merchants, fearing that Thatcherton was going to get Hopkinville's railroad." This is a sentence fragment, so ZAP F. You can ZAP G because the subject—the town's merchants—has already been stated and does not have to be restated with "they." J is incorrect because a semicolon can only separate two independent clauses, and the first part of the sentence is a dependent clause. H is the most reasonable answer.

31-A The verb tense is correct as is. B is definitely wrong because "could of" is an incorrect way of saying "could have." C and D force an incorrect tense.

32-J Whole-paragraph question. F is not correct, for little emphasis is put on the writer's grandfather. G and H are not correct, because the first paragraph answers these questions. J is correct, because we don't know why the railroad barely made its deadline.

33-C The words "So that" make the sentence following the period a run-on sentence. B also creates a run-on sentence. For D to be correct, it would require a comma between "night" and "and."

34-G Two sentences are incorrectly connected with "and." If the two sentences were closely related, a comma would go before "and," but since they are not, they should be two separate sentences with no conjunctions (*and, but, so, or*) between them.

35-B This question asks you to think about the writer's tone. The author intends to be slightly humorous and noncommittal about certain parts of the celebration. The reader should not take everything the author is saying literally.

36-F The sentence is important and should be kept because it brings the story to a conclusion after so much uncertainty. It also leads smoothly into the details of the party that the writer describes.

37-A Simple writing is best. Answers B and D invite you to use complicated punctuation for no apparent reason, and C creates a sentence fragment: "But when I close my eyes, as she did when telling the story to me" is an incomplete sentence.

38-J A sentence fragment follows the period. G is too long. H uses a semicolon incorrectly.

39-B "Their fathers'" is the correct form of the possessive since more than one boy is sitting on the shoulders of more than one father.

40-G The phrase, "decked out in their finest dresses," modifies "ladies of Hopkinville." This kind of modifier is preceded by a comma, a symbol for a natural pause. Omitting the underlined portion would remove a vivid description.

41-B The essay discusses the coming of the railroad to Hopkinville via the writer's personal connection to the event. In the last paragraph, the writer imagines the scene on the day the first train arrived in Hopkinville. The last sentence is appropriate in that context.

English Answer Review
Workout F

1-A The sentence is correct. "Administering medicines" occurs in the present and "requires" is the correct present-tense form of the verb.

2-J The phrase beginning with "your good judgment but" needs to better imply the contrast between "good judgment" and "ability to relate to children as people." The word "but" is your clue that the sentence is awkward. "Both" (G) does not support this contrast. "More than your" (H) sounds good but changes the meaning. It would imply that your ability to relate to children as people is a greater asset than your good judgment. Whether this is true or not, the author did not mean to say this; so by choosing J, the author's meaning is preserved.

3-A Since "of course" can be removed from the sentence without any loss, it should be set off with commas. "Assuredly" means the same as "of course," but B is missing the comma.

4-G If you read just the subject and verb, the sentence says "a young person will be resisting taking medicine." The verb is "will be resisting taking," which sounds awkward. "Will resist taking medicine" sounds more natural.

5-D Shorter is better. Rarely does a writer need to say "thing." Choices A, B, and C retain the wordiness of the original sentence.

6-F The essay is written in second person, addressing the reader as "you." "One" is the formal, third-person way of addressing the reader and is inconsistent with the more casual tone of the essay.

7-C Answer C is the most specific statement. It gives the reader the most clear image of what the writer means by saying "manner, words, and tone of voice should all convey a positive attitude."

8-H Look at the skeleton of the sentence. The simplest form of the sentence says, "you should respond to questions." Looking at it this way, you should see that only "truthfully" (H) adequately completes the sentence. G adds an unnecessary period after the question mark and uses a semicolon incorrectly by ending the fragment "And truthfully" as if it were an independent clause. J is wordy and uses a semicolon where a comma is appropriate.

9-D The words "will to some extent grow" mean as much as "will grow," so "to some extent" can be deleted. B and C achieve the same effect as "to some extent."

10-J Your clue that the sentence can be improved is that "Or" and "however" are in the same sentence. Paragraph breaks are intended to put a piece of writing into bite-size pieces for the reader. Inserting a new paragraph here is logical because the discussion is changing from distasteful medicine to pleasant-tasting medicine.

11-D The sentence has two verbs where it only needs one: "are" (in the contraction "They're") and "can be." Only D removes one of the extra verbs.

12-H The introductory phrase is "For very young children." This type of phrase is set off with a comma. Possessives are not the issue (F and J). Semicolons don't set off phrases that aren't complete clauses (G).

13-B "Secretly" and "camouflage strategies" are redundant, and inserting a period creates a fragment. Only B corrects the redundancy and correctly connects the two parts of the sentence. Notice that even though a comma doesn't have to precede "but" in this sentence, writers often use one to emphasize the contrast.

14-G Shorter is better. All the answers mean the same thing, but G uses fewer words.

15-A The question invites you to change the punctuation around the modifier "even those who show a great deal of resistance." Since this modifier ends with a comma, it should begin with a comma.

16-H Whole-passage question. You are being asked to describe the author's audience in writing this essay. The content suggests that it is not for someone who often administers medicine. This rules out doctors and nurses. J can be ruled out because the passage makes no special mention of how to deal with children in a hospital.

17-B Run-on sentence. The comma between "principal" and "he" creates a run-on sentence spliced by a comma. It is important to recognize that the phrase "refused to allow . . ." is critically describing the principal in question. The semicolon (D) is not the best choice because it will separate "principal" from "refused to allow. . . ." Both "who" (B) and "that" (C) will connect the phrase, but "who" is correct because the phrase refers to a person.

18-F The sentence is correct. The answer choices invite you to change the verb form (G and J) or insert commas between the subject and verb (H and J).

19-C The paragraph speaks of the principal's objections in the past tense: "Motivating him were," "he believed," and "he feared." The verb "feel" should be in the past tense: "felt."

20-F This is the correct form of the plural possessive, since there is more than one student involved. G makes the sentence wordy. H and J are incorrect possessives.

21-C The antecedent of "they" is unclear. "They" refers to "the articles" but since a reader can mistake "they" to mean people, it is preferable to be more exact.

22-G You can best understand the principal's motivation through his words or actions, rather than imagining his probable reactions to the situations described in F, H, and J. G is the only answer that directly refers to the principal's actions.

23-D As written, the sentence contains a run-on sentence spliced by a comma. The phrase following the comma contains "which," making the phrase dependent on the preceding words, so B and C won't work. D removes the comma, creating a complete and smooth phrase: "in agreement with a lower court, which had previously ruled in favor of the students."

24-H This sentence contains a dangling modifier. The sentence begins with, "Arguing that the student newspaper," but the subject is "the newspaper." The sentence means that the newspaper is arguing that the student newspaper is a public forum. This is not true; the lower court argued that it was a public forum. Only H uses the correct subject.

25-A The sentence is correct. This sentence is similar to "I thought that you were right." You would not put a comma after "thought."

26-G The phrase beginning with "That students in American public schools" can be introduced with a colon or a dash. Whether to use a dash or colon is the writer's choice, so the ACT will not force you to choose between a dash or colon unless both are wrong answers.

27-B The correct way to finish this sentence is to say "adults do" or "adults." Only one of these is offered as an answer. Notice that two of the incorrect answers (C and D) tempt you to use different — but still incorrect — possessive forms.

28-F The paragraph is explaining how the court decided that students have rights as adults. When arguing a point or illustrating an example, essays cite facts and examples. F is an example that fits in with how the Court views students' rights.

English Answer Review Workout F

29-C   The sentence is incorrect as written, because the comma after "then" is not needed. The words "in fact" and "therefore" also followed by commas are no better than "then," for they mean the same thing. "However" is a word that sets up a contrast. The viewpoint of saying "no" in this paragraph is being contrasted with saying "yes" in the previous paragraph. "However" strengthens this contrast and is always separated with commas.

30-J   This is a question that comes up often on the ACT. There is nothing really wrong with any of the choices. You simply have to use your ear to pick the right response.

31-C   To choose the correct word, you need to read the whole sentence. The word "charting" was used. One charts a "course," not an "attitude," "view," or "viewpoint."

32-J   As it is written, the sentence refers to "the Court" as "they," which is incorrect. G is incorrect because "it's" means "it is." H is incorrect because "they're" means "they are." J is correct; implicit in "the belief" is the knowledge that the belief is "the Court's."

33-B   Whole-passage question. Sentence 4 is a general statement. Sentence 1 speaks of the Court's more conservative view, and sentence 4 says what was underlying this view. Both sentences are a prelude to the more specific descriptions in sentences 2 and 3.

34-G   The first two paragraphs say, "Imagine that you are a member of the Supreme Court" and "the case reaches you for a decision." Saying that "your decision will have lasting consequences" encourages you to take the task more seriously, so you will read paragraphs 3 and 4 more carefully.

> Life is not a rehearsal, so whatever you choose to do, it is good if your heart is in it.
> —Mireille Guiliano

Mathematics Answer Review
Workout A

1-C Fred owns one more book than the average of the other three. The average of the other three is their sum divided by 3.

$$\frac{22 + 17 + 24}{3} = \frac{63}{3} = 21$$

Remember, Fred has one more, so he has $21 + 1 = 22$.

2-J To find the decimal value of $\frac{20}{19}$ divide 20 by 19.

$$\begin{array}{r} 1.05 \\ 19\overline{)20} \\ \underline{19} \\ 100 \\ \underline{95} \\ 5 \end{array}$$

The closest answer is 1.05. Since $\frac{20}{19}$ has to be greater than 1, you can quickly ZAP A and B, which are both less than 1. Since $\frac{20}{19}$ is greater than 1.05, you can ZAP C as well because 1.02 is less than 1.05.

3-D The perimeter of a square is 4 times the length of a side or $4x$. The area of a square is the length of a side squared or x^2. You are told in the problem that the area is $4x + 12$, so you can set $4x + 12$ equal to x^2.

$$x^2 = 4x + 12$$

$x^2 - 4x - 12 = 0$ Subtract $4x$ and 12 from each side.

$(x - 6)(x + 2) = 0$ Factor.

$x - 6 = 0$ OR $x + 2 = 0$

$x = 6$ OR $x = -2$ The length of the side can't be negative, so 6 is the length of the side.

The perimeter is $4 \cdot 6$ or 24.

Mathematics Answer Review Workout A

4-G The question asks for the length of the motorboat. Since the yacht is 40 feet longer than the motorboat, if you add 40 to the length of the motorboat it will equal the length of the yacht.

$$(m + 5) + 40 = 2m^2$$
$$m + 45 = 2m^2$$

Since this is a quadratic equation, subtract terms from both sides to get an equation with zero on one side and then factor.

$$2m^2 - m - 45 = 0$$
$$(2m + 9)(m - 5) = 0$$
$$2m + 9 = 0 \quad \text{OR} \quad m - 5 = 0$$
$$m = -\frac{9}{2} \quad \text{OR} \quad m = 5$$

The length must be positive so $m = 5$. The length of the motorboat is $m + 5$.

$$5 + 5 = 10$$

5-E The two right triangles are congruent by the Hypotenuse-Leg theorem. $\angle CAB$ has the same measure as $\angle DCA$ because they are corresponding parts of congruent triangles. Since $\angle DCA$ and $\angle ACE$ make a straight line they add up to $180°$. $\angle DCA = 180° - 131° = 49°$, so the measure of $\angle CAB$ is $49°$.

6-K This problem expects you to know $\sin^2 \theta + \cos^2 \theta = 1$.

$$\frac{1}{\sin^2 \theta + \cos^2 \theta} = \frac{1}{1} = 1$$

7-B Let r = radius of the circle. The rectangle has a length of $2r$ and a width of r. The area is 18, so you can solve for r.

$$(2r)(r) = 18$$
$$2r^2 = 18 \quad \quad \text{Divide by 2.}$$
$$r^2 = 9 \quad \quad \text{Take the square root.}$$
$$r = 3$$

The area of a circle is πr^2. Substitute $r = 3$.

$$A = \pi(3)^2$$
$$A = 9\pi$$

8-J To find out how much the customers will pay, first find out how many baseballs were sold. Divide the total profit of $17.00 by the profit on each of $0.85 to find out how many baseballs were sold.

$$.85\overline{)17.00}$$
quotient 20, with 17.00 − 17.00 = 00

If the customers buy 20 baseballs at $4.50 each, the total amount they will pay is $20 \times 4.50 = \$90$.

9-B Jane is paid $110x$ for the first 110 subscriptions. She still needs to be paid for the other 5 subscriptions. She is paid $5 \cdot 2x = 10x$ for those 5 subscriptions since she is paid twice as much for each of them. Altogether, she is paid $110x + 10x = 120x$.

10-F x more than m is $m + x$.

x less than $2m$ is $2m - x$.

To get the product, multiply:

$(m + x)(2m - x)$

$= 2m^2 - mx + 2mx - x^2$ Add the middle terms.

$= 2m^2 + mx - x^2$

11-C If segment AB is inside the circle, then it must be shorter than the diameter. The diameter is the distance all the way across the circle through the center and is twice the radius. The radius is 2 so the diameter is 4. $AB < 4$.

12-H To find out how many flowers 5 people can make in 10 hours, first find out how many they can make in 1 hour, then multiply that number times 10.

In 1 hour: $\dfrac{100 \text{ flowers}}{8 \text{ people}} = \dfrac{x}{5 \text{ people}}$

$8x = 500$

$x = \dfrac{500}{8}$ OR 62.5

In 10 hours: $62.5 \cdot 10 = 625$ flowers.

13-A $\overline{BC}$ is the side opposite $\angle A$ and $\overline{AB}$ is the hypotenuse. The sin function uses those two sides.

$\sin = \dfrac{\text{opposite}}{\text{hypotenuse}}$ Substitute 10 for the hypotenuse, 0.669 for the sin 42°, and $\overline{BC}$ for the side opposite.

$0.669 = \dfrac{BC}{10}$ Multiply by 10.

$\overline{BC} = 6.69$

Note: The hypotenuse of a right triangle is the longest side so you can *ZAP* D and E.

Mathematics Answer Review Workout A

14-H The area of a triangle is one half of the base times the height. If you use side $\overline{CB}$ as the base, then $\overline{AC}$ is the height. $\overline{CB}$ is y units long, and you can use the Pythagorean Theorem to find $\overline{AC}$.

$$(\overline{AC})^2 = x^2 - y^2$$

$$\overline{AC} = \sqrt{x^2 - y^2}$$

$$\text{Area} = \tfrac{1}{2} y \sqrt{x^2 - y^2} \quad \text{OR} \quad \tfrac{y}{2}\sqrt{x^2 - y^2}$$

15-D $84 = 2 \times 42$, but 42 is not prime, so factor it.

$84 = 2 \times 6 \times 7$, but 6 is not prime, so factor it.

$84 = 2 \times 2 \times 3 \times 7$ Now all factors are prime.

You can ZAP A, B, and C because the answers contain numbers that are not prime.

16-F The area of a triangle is one half of the base times the height. In this problem, the base is $2a - b$, and the height is $2a + 2b$, so:

$$\text{Area} = \tfrac{1}{2}(2a - b)(2a + 2b) \quad\quad \text{Foil the two factors.}$$

$$= \tfrac{1}{2}(4a^2 + 4ab - 2ab - 2b^2) \quad\quad \text{Combine the middle terms.}$$

$$= \tfrac{1}{2}(4a^2 + 2ab - 2b^2) \quad\quad \text{Multiply by } \tfrac{1}{2}.$$

$$= 2a^2 + ab - b^2$$

17-A
$i(2i + 9) = x - i$	Multiply by the i.
$2i^2 + 9i = x - i$	Add i to each side.
$2i^2 + 10i = x$	Replace i^2 with -1.
$2(-1) + 10i = x$	Multiply by the 2.
$-2 + 10i = x$	Rearrange the terms.
$10i - 2 = x$	

18-K Subtract 2 from both sides of the equation to get $5x^2 + 3x - 2 = 0$. Substitute $a = 5$, $b = 3$, and $c = -2$.

$$b^2 - 4ac = 3^2 - 4(5)(-2)$$

$$= 9 + 40$$

$$= 49$$

19-E Since the choices are so close together, you can't tell which choice is correct by looking at the graph. By using intercepts (0, 6) and (5, 0), you can find the equation of the line.

The slope $= \frac{6-0}{0-5} = -\frac{6}{5}$ so the equation in slope intercept form is $y = -\frac{6}{5}x + b$.

To solve for b, substitute the coordinate pair (0, 6) for (x, y).

$$y = -\frac{6}{5}x + b$$

$$6 = -\frac{6}{5}(0) + b$$

$$6 = b$$

The equation is $y = -\frac{6}{5}x + 6$.

Substitute 2 for x and p for y to find the correct value of p.

$$p = -\frac{6}{5}(2) + 6$$

$$p = -\frac{12}{5} + 6$$

$$p = -\frac{12}{5} + \frac{30}{5}$$

$$p = \frac{18}{5}$$

$$p = 3\frac{3}{5}$$

20-G The slopes of two perpendicular lines are negative reciprocals. The equation of line $q\left(y = \frac{3}{2}x + 2\right)$ is given in slope-intercept form. The slope of line q is $\frac{3}{2}$ and the slope of line k is $-\frac{2}{3}$. In slope-intercept form, line k has the equation $y = -\frac{2}{3}x + b$ where b is the y-intercept.

To find b, substitute the point (2, 2) into the equation, and solve for b.

$$2 = -\frac{2}{3}(2) + b$$

$$2 = -\frac{4}{3} + b$$

$$2 + \frac{4}{3} = b$$

$$\frac{6}{3} + \frac{4}{3} = b$$

$$b = \frac{10}{3}$$

Mathematics Answer Review Workout B

1-D You can simplify what is inside the parentheses first. Remember that when you multiply powers of the same base, you add the exponents.

$$(3y \cdot 4y^2 \cdot y^3)^2 = (12y^6)^2$$
$$= (12y^6)(12y^6)$$
$$= 144y^{12}$$

2-J In a geometric sequence, each term is obtained from the previous term by multiplying by a common ratio, r. In this case, the common ratio is $-\frac{1}{2}$: $4 \cdot -\frac{1}{2} = -2$, $-2 \cdot -\frac{1}{2} = 1$; and $1 \cdot -\frac{1}{2} = -\frac{1}{2}$. Continuing to multiply by $-\frac{1}{2}$, we find that the fifth term of the sequence is $\frac{1}{4}$, the sixth term is $-\frac{1}{8}$, the seventh term is $\frac{1}{16}$, and the eighth term is $-\frac{1}{32}$.

3-B Since $\triangle ABC$ is a right triangle, use the Pythagorean Theorem to solve for side $\overline{CB}$:

$(AC)^2 + (CB)^2 = (AB)^2$

$(4)^2 + (CB)^2 = (8)^2$ Square.

$16 + (CB)^2 = 64$ Subtract 16.

$(CB)^2 = 48$ Take square root.

$(CB) = \sqrt{48}$ Simplify.

$(CB) = \sqrt{16} \cdot \sqrt{3}$

$(CB) = 4 \cdot \sqrt{3}$

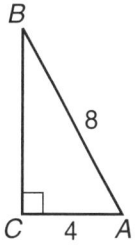

4-J The center of the circle is the midpoint of the diameter. To find the midpoint of $\overline{AB}$, find the average of the x-coordinates and the average of the y-coordinates.

$$\left(\frac{-1+3}{2}, \frac{5+5}{2}\right) = \left(\frac{2}{2}, \frac{10}{2}\right) = (1, 5)$$

Note: You could also plot the points given as choices on the graph. Since both A and B are on the horizontal line $y = 5$, the y-coordinate of the center must also be 5. You can ZAP G and H. Since K has the same coordinates as A, you can ZAP K.

5-A Since the greater answer must be greater for all numbers $x > 1$, you just need to pick any number greater than 1, and substitute it in each equation. The greatest number will be the correct answer. Set $x = 2$.

    A. $\dfrac{2+1}{2-1} = \dfrac{3}{1} = 3$

    B. $\dfrac{2-1}{2+1} = \dfrac{1}{3}$

    C. $\dfrac{2}{2+1} = \dfrac{2}{3}$

    D. $\dfrac{2}{2-1} = 2$

    E. $\dfrac{2-1}{2} = \dfrac{1}{2}$

$\dfrac{x+1}{x-1}$ will have the greater value for all $x > 1$.

6-H There are four geometry facts that you need to know to work this problem.

One angle of the triangle measures 90° because this is a right triangle. The measures of the other two angles add up to 90° because the sum of the measures of all the angles of a triangle must be 180°. Each of those two angles measures 45° because in an isosceles triangle at least two angles have equal measures. That means $\angle PRQ$ has a measure of 45°. $\angle PRS$ has a measure of $180 - 45 = 135$ because, together, those two angles form a line.

7-E The large numbers in this problem make it hard to factor or use the quadratic formula. Subtract 22 from both sides to get an equation with zero on one side by itself.

$6y^2 + 29y - 22 = 0$ Factor.

$(3y - 2)(2y + 11) = 0$

$3y - 2 = 0$ OR $2y + 11 = 0$ Solve each equation for y.

$3y = 2$ $2y = -11$

$y = \dfrac{2}{3}$ $y = -\dfrac{11}{2}$

The only answer given in the choices is $\dfrac{2}{3}$.

Note: If $6y^2 + 29y - 22 = 0$, then $6y^2 + 29y$ would have to equal 22. Therefore, y has to be less than 1.

8-H To get $|f(-2)|$ substitute -2 for a in the equation $f(a) = a^2 + 4a$, and take the absolute value of the answer.

$|f(-2)| = |(-2)^2 + 4(-2)|$
$= |4 - 8|$
$= |-4|$
$= 4$

Mathematics Answer Review Workout B

9-E The question asks for the sum of the measures of $\angle ABE$ and $\angle DCE$. $\angle DCE$ has the same measure as $\angle ABE$ because when two parallel lines are cut by a transversal, alternate interior angles are congruent. $\angle AEB$ measures $40°$ because together with $\angle DEB$ they make a line. $\angle EAB$ measures $90°$. $\angle ABE$ measures $180° - 90° - 40° = 50°$ because the sum of the measures of the three angles of a triangle is $180°$. Since $\angle DCE$ has the same measure as $\angle ABE$. They each measure $50°$, and their sum is $100°$.

10-F Look at the format of the choices given. To get the expression in that form, factor it. The greatest common factor of the two terms is $4xy^2$. Factoring $4xy^2$ out of the $8x^2y^2$ leaves $2x$, and factoring $4xy^2$ out of $-4xy^3$ leaves $-y$. So the correct factorization is $4xy^2(2x - y)$.

Note: You could find the correct choice by multiplying each of the choices together to see which one matches the expression $8x^2y^2 - 4xy^3$ from the question. If you did that, the correct products would be:

F. $4xy^2(2x - y) = 8x^2y^2 - 4xy^3$

G. $4x^2y^2(2 - y) = 8x^2y^2 - 4x^2y^3$

H. $4xy(2x - y) = 8x^2y - 4xy^2$

J. $4xy(2xy - 2y^2) = 8x^2y^2 - 8xy^3$

K. $2xy^2(4x - 2) = 8x^2y^2 - 4xy^2$

11-D Perhaps the easiest way to solve this question is to use the triangle determined by the three cities.

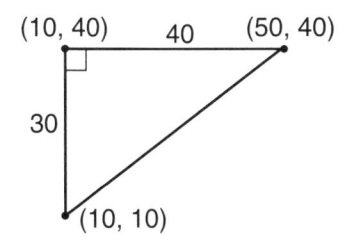

This triangle will be a right triangle with legs of 30 and 40 miles.

Therefore, $30^2 + 40^2 = x^2$ (These numbers are multiples of
$900 + 1600 = x^2$ the 3-4-5 Pythagorean triple.)
$2500 = x^2$
$50 = x$

Note: You could also use the distance formula:

$d = \sqrt{(x_1 - x_2)^2 + (y_1 - y_2)^2}$

$d = \sqrt{(50 - 10)^2 + (40 - 10)^2}$

$= \sqrt{40^2 + 30^2}$

$= \sqrt{1600 + 900}$

$= \sqrt{2500}$

$= 50$

12-F The total mileage for the trip is 100.

100 ÷ 21 ≈ 4.76 gallons of gas used

4.76 × 2.20 = $10.47

The correct answer is F, $10.

13-B Find the midpoint of the segment determined by the points (10, 10) and (50, 40).

$$\text{Midpoint} = \left(\frac{x_1 + x_2}{2}, \frac{y_1 + y_2}{2}\right)$$

$$= \left(\frac{10 + 50}{2}, \frac{10 + 40}{2}\right)$$

$$= \left(\frac{60}{2}, \frac{50}{2}\right)$$

$$= (30, 25)$$

14-K Translate the words in the problem into an equation, and solve for x. x is the number of pencils in the box. "Multiply x by 5 and decrease the result by 8" is the expression $5x - 8$. "3 times a number that is 2 greater than x" is the expression $3(x + 2)$. The problem says that the two expressions are equal.

$5x - 8 = 3(x + 2)$	Simplify.
$5x - 8 = 3x + 6$	Add 8 to both sides.
$5x = 3x + 14$	Subtract $3x$ from both sides.
$2x = 14$	Divide by 2.
$x = 7$	

15-D The function $f(x)$ yields a positive output for any real number input x. Since $g(x)$ will always be a real number regardless of x, when $g(x)$ is input into the function $f(x)$, the result must always be positive.

16-F By looking at the choices, you can see that the format is the same as the solutions that come from the quadratic formula.

$$x = \frac{-b \pm \sqrt{b^2 - 4ac}}{2a}$$

The only difference between the two answers given by the quadratic formula is the plus or minus sign in the numerator. The solution given in the problem is $\frac{-3 + \sqrt{2}}{2}$, so the other one must be $\frac{-3 - \sqrt{2}}{2}$.

Mathematics Answer Review Workout B

17-C The question asks for the area of the triangle. Since the base is given in terms of the height, and the height is given in terms of the base, the height (h) and the base (b) can be found with two equations. The two equations are $b = h - 4.5$ and $h = 2b + 1$. If you substitute what h is equal to in the second equation into the first equation, you can find b.

$b = (2b + 1) - 4.5$

$b = 2b - 3.5$

$b = 3.5$

Now substitute 3.5 for b in the second equation to find h.

$h = 2(3.5) + 1$

$h = 7 + 1$

$h = 8$

The area of a triangle equals $\frac{1}{2}bh$.

$\frac{1}{2}(3.5)(8) = 14$.

18-G The question says that one angle of a triangle measures $x°$ and asks for the sum of the other two angles. Since the sum of all three angles of a triangle equals 180°, the sum of the remaining two angles is $(180 - x)°$.

19-B $x - \frac{7x}{3} > -1$ Multiply both sides by 3. Combine the x terms.

$3x - 7x > -3$

$-4x > -3$ Divide by -4.

$x < \frac{3}{4}$ Reverse the inequality sign.

20-K Neither of the first two choices simplifies, and neither of them is equal to y^{27}, so simplify the last 3 choices.

H. $(9y)^3 = 9^3 \cdot y^3 = 729y^3$

J. $(y^9)^2 = y^{18}$ (Remember that you multiply exponents when you have a power to a power.)

K. $(y^9)^3 = y^{27}$

Mathematics Answer Review
Workout C

1-D 40% of the 50 members support the tax increase. To find out how many members that is, multiply .40 times 50.

$$.40 \times 50 = 20$$

80% of this group of 20 members believe the increase will pass. To find out how many members are in this group, multiply .80 times 20.

$$.80 \times 20 = 16$$

2-H Since $\triangle ACE$ is an equilateral triangle, each angle measures 60°. The three altitudes each form two 30-60-90 triangles. The 6 small non-overlaping triangles that share G as a vertex will also be 30-60-90 triangles, and will have equal areas. Therefore, the ratio of the area of $\triangle CGD$ to the area of $\triangle CFE$ will be 1:3.

3-A
$4a + 4 = 11$ Subtract 4.

$4a = 11 - 4$ Divide by 4.

$a = \frac{11 - 4}{4}$

4-K To solve the inequality, follow these steps:

$4x + 7 < -17$ Subtract 7 from each side.

$4x < -24$ Divide each side by 4.

$x < -6$

5-C How far the point is from the y-axis is determined by how far the x-coordinate (or first coordinate) is from zero. Point A is 3 units away. Points B, D, and E are each 2 units away. Point C is only 1 unit away.

6-J The formula for the circumference of a circle is $C = 2\pi r$. In this problem, $16 = 2\pi r$, so $8 = \pi r$ and $r = \frac{8}{\pi}$.

7-E To solve an equation with a radical in it, first get the radical on one side of the equation by itself.

$\sqrt{x - 5} - x = -5$ Add x to each side.

$\sqrt{x - 5} = x - 5$ Square each side.

$x - 5 = x^2 - 10x + 25$ Subtract to get zero on one side.

$x^2 - 11x + 30 = 0$ Factor.

$(x - 6)(x - 5) = 0$

$x - 6 = 0$ OR $x - 5 = 0$

$x = 6$ OR $x = 5$

6 is the only answer given.

Note: The correct answer to this question can also be found by plugging in the choices for x. The only one that doesn't yield a negative under the radical is 6.

8-G Let's start with the first fact: $\cos\left(\frac{\pi}{2}\right) = 0$. From the graph, we can see that $\sin \pi = 0$, so in this case at least, since $\pi - \frac{\pi}{2} = \frac{\pi}{2}$, it follows that $\sin x = \cos\left(x - \frac{\pi}{2}\right)$. Turning our attention to the second fact, $\cos \pi = -1$, we can see on the graph that $\sin \frac{3\pi}{2} = -1$, so again, since $\frac{3\pi}{2} - \frac{\pi}{2} = \pi$, we have $\sin x = \cos\left(x - \frac{\pi}{2}\right)$.

9-B If the ratio of boys to girls is $x:9$, then there is some number, n, that allows you to take x times n to get the number of boys and 9 times n to get the number of girls. The total of the boys plus the girls must equal 500.

$$xn = \text{number of boys}$$

$$9n = \text{number of girls}$$

$$xn + 9n = 500 \qquad \text{Now solve for } n \text{ in terms of } x.$$

$$(x + 9)n = 500$$

$$n = \frac{500}{x + 9}$$

The question asks for the number of girls ($9n$).

$$9n = 9\left(\frac{500}{x + 9}\right), \text{ which is the same as } 500\left(\frac{9}{x + 9}\right).$$

10-F To find the equation of a line through two points, first find the slope. The slope equals the change in y divided by the change in x.

$$\frac{6 - 1}{1 - (-4)} = \frac{5}{5} = 1 \qquad \text{Use the point } (1, 6) \text{ and the slope to simplify the equation.}$$

$$y - y_1 = m(x - x_1)$$

$$y - 6 = 1(x - 1)$$

$$y - 6 = x - 1$$

$$y - x = 5$$

11-D One of the numbers is $x + 2$ and the other is $x - 3$. The sum is $x + 2 + x - 3$ or $2x - 1$. The problem says that the sum is 11, so $2x - 1 = 11$ is the correct equation.

12-K

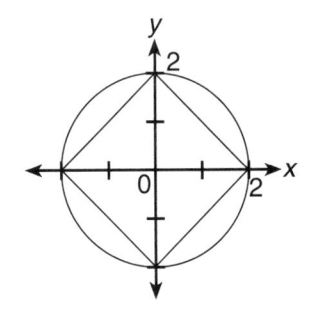

Draw a picture to see what the square looks like. To find the perimeter, you first need to find the length of a side of the square. To find the length of a side, use one of the right triangles and the Pythagorean Theorem. The hypotenuse of the triangle will be the length of one side of the square. The side of the square = $\sqrt{2^2 + 2^2} = \sqrt{4 + 4} = \sqrt{8} = 2\sqrt{2}$. Since the perimeter is four times the length of a side, $4(2\sqrt{2}) = 8\sqrt{2}$.

13-C To find the intersection of two lines, multiply one equation by some number so that when you add the other equation (or some multiple of it) one of the variables drops out. $-2(2x + y = -1) = -4x - 2y = 2$. Add the two equations.

$$
\begin{aligned}
3x + 2y &= -2 \\
+ -4x - 2y &= 2 \\
\hline
-x &= 0 \quad \text{OR} \quad x = 0
\end{aligned}
$$

Plug in 0 for x in one of the equations.

$2(0) + y = -1 \quad \text{OR} \quad y = -1$

Note: You could find the correct choice by plugging each point into one equation. If it doesn't work, ZAP it and, if it does, plug it into the other equation because it must work in both.

14-G

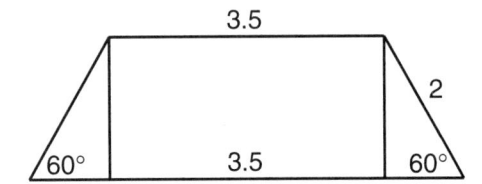

Since both base angles are the same, the two legs of the trapezoid are both 2. To find the length of the longer base, draw two lines to the base to make a rectangle and two 30°−60°−90° triangles. In a 30°−60°−90° triangle, the short leg is one half of the hypotenuse. Since the hypotenuse is 2, the short leg is 1. The long base of the trapezoid is $3.5 + 1 + 1 = 5.5$. The perimeter of the trapezoid is $5.5 + 2 + 2 + 3.5 = 13$.

15-B $5.97 \times 10^{24} - 7.35 \times 10^{22} =$

$597.0 \times 10^{22} - 7.35 \times 10^{22} = 589.65 \times 10^{22}$

which is approximately

$5.8965 \times 10^{24} \approx 5.9 \times 10^{24}$

Mathematics Answer Review Workout C

16-H Since the problem gives you the sin $x = \frac{1}{3}$ and asks for the cos x, you can use the identity:

$$\sin^2 x + \cos^2 x = 1$$

$$\left(\frac{1}{3}\right)^2 + \cos^2 x = 1 \qquad \text{Square } \frac{1}{3}.$$

$$\frac{1}{9} + \cos^2 x = 1 \qquad \text{Subtract } \frac{1}{9}.$$

$$\cos^2 x = \frac{8}{9} \qquad \text{Take the square root of each side.}$$

$$\cos x = \frac{\sqrt{8}}{\sqrt{9}} \qquad \text{Substitute 3 for } \sqrt{9}.$$

$$\cos x = \frac{\sqrt{8}}{3}$$

17-E $(-3)^2 - (-2)^2 = 9 - 4 = 5$

18-H $x > \frac{1}{2}x + 10$

$\frac{1}{2}x > 10$

$x > 20$

Since $x > 20$, there are 4 values less than 25 that can equal x. {21, 22, 23, 24}.

19-A The ratios mean that for every 4 apples there is 1 orange, and that for every 4 apples there are 7 peaches. That means for every 1 orange there are 7 peaches, and the ratio of oranges to peaches is 1:7.

20-J A and B each have a y-coordinate of 4. Since $\overline{AB}$ is a diameter, the center of the circle is on the same horizontal line $y = 4$ and has a y-coordinate of 4. The distance between A and B is the diameter of the circle. The diameter is equal to 5, and the radius is one half the diameter or 2.5. The point on the circle with the largest y-coordinate is straight up from the center, a distance of 2.5. The y-coordinate of the point asked for is $4 + 2.5 = 6.5$.

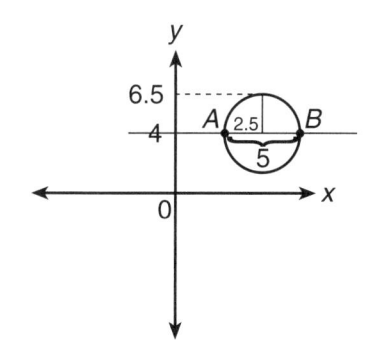

Mathematics Answer Review
Workout D

1-A First off, because the inequality is strictly less than, as opposed to less than or equal to, both lines should be dashed, eliminating choices B, D, and E. From there, it's best to think of this as two separate graphs. Ignoring the 4 gives us $0 < 2x + y$, or $-2x < y$. Ignoring the 0 gives us $2x + y < 4$, or $y < 4 - 2x$. Graphing $y > -2x$ and $y < 4 - 2x$ gives us choice A.

2-J Since $a = b$, replace b with a in each equation and simplify both sides to see if they match.

F. $(\sqrt{a + a})^2 = 2a^2$
$(\sqrt{a + a})^2 = 2a^2$
$(\sqrt{2a})^2 = 2a^2$
$2a = 2a^2$
Not True

G. $\sqrt{a} \cdot \sqrt{b} = \dfrac{b}{a}$
$\sqrt{a} \cdot \sqrt{a} = \dfrac{a}{a}$
$\sqrt{a^2} = 1$
$a = 1$
Not True

H. $\dfrac{1}{\sqrt{a}} \cdot \dfrac{1}{\sqrt{b}} = \dfrac{1}{2ab}$
$\dfrac{1}{\sqrt{a}} \cdot \dfrac{1}{\sqrt{a}} = \dfrac{1}{2a \cdot a}$
$\dfrac{1}{\sqrt{a^2}} = \dfrac{1}{2a^2}$
$\dfrac{1}{a} = \dfrac{1}{2a^2}$
Not True

J. $\dfrac{\sqrt{(a)^b}}{\sqrt{(b)^a}} = \dfrac{a}{b}$
$\dfrac{\sqrt{a^a}}{\sqrt{a^a}} = \dfrac{a}{a}$
$1 = 1$
True

K. $\sqrt{ab} \cdot \sqrt{ab} = ab^2$
$\sqrt{a \cdot a} \cdot \sqrt{a \cdot a} = a \cdot a^2$
$\sqrt{a^2} \cdot \sqrt{a^2} = a^3$
$a \cdot a = a^3$
$a^2 = a^3$
Not True

Mathematics Answer Review Workout D

3-B   To solve a quadratic equation, set the equation equal to zero and factor.

$$11x - 2x^2 = 5 \qquad \text{Add } 2x^2 \text{ to both sides.}$$

$$11x = 2x^2 + 5 \qquad \text{Subtract } 11x \text{ from both sides.}$$

$$0 = 2x^2 - 11x + 5 \quad \text{OR} \quad 2x^2 - 11x + 5 = 0 \qquad \text{Factor.}$$

$$(2x - 1)(x - 5) = 0$$

$$2x - 1 = 0 \quad \text{OR} \quad x - 5 = 0$$

$$2x = 1$$

$$x = \tfrac{1}{2} \quad \text{OR} \quad x = 5$$

Note: You could ZAP A, C, and E by substituting the 1.

4-K   To find miles per hour, divide miles by hours.

$$\frac{14r^2 + 21rs}{7r} = \frac{7r(2r + 3s)}{7r} = 2r + 3s$$

Note: Since you know that to get miles per hour you divide, you can ZAP F because the items are subtracted and G because they are multiplied.

5-D $(2 + 3\sqrt{3})(1 - \sqrt{3})$ F.O.I.L. (First–Outer–Inner–Last)

$\quad\quad\quad = 2(1) + 2(-\sqrt{3}) + 3\sqrt{3}(1) + 3\sqrt{3}(-\sqrt{3})$ Multiply the parts.

$\quad\quad\quad = 2 - 2\sqrt{3} + 3\sqrt{3} - 9$ Combine like terms.

$\quad\quad\quad = -7 + \sqrt{3}$

$\quad\quad\quad = \sqrt{3} - 7$

6-H   112

The list of numbers, from lesser to greater is:

        92, 98, 100, 106, 112, 120, 130, 180, 180

The median is 112.

7-E   115

Set up a proportion:

80 is to 100, as 92 is to x.

$\frac{80}{100} = \frac{92}{x}$

$80x = 9200$

$\quad x = 115$

Another way: 80% of $x = 92$

$$.80x = 92$$

$$x = \frac{92}{.80}$$

$$x = 115$$

8-G 3 numbers in the list fall between 50 and 100. 4 numbers in the list fall between 101 and 150. 2 numbers in the list fall between 151 and 200.

9-B To find the average of the new list, which contains 3 additional numbers (x, y, and z), you must add x, y, and z to the sum of the 9 original numbers and divide by 12.

10-J There are 360° in a circle. This arc of 8 inches is the same part of the circumference that the 40° angle is out of the 360° for the whole circle. Using c as the circumference, this can be written as a proportion.

$$\frac{40}{360} = \frac{8}{c}$$ Simplify $\frac{40}{360}$ to $\frac{1}{9}$.

$$\frac{1}{9} = \frac{8}{c}$$ Cross multiply.

$$c = 72$$

Since the circumference of a circle equals π times the diameter, substitute πd for c.

$$\pi d = 72$$ Divide by π.

$$d = \frac{72}{\pi}$$

11-B To find the average cost per item, take the total cost divided by the number of items. The cost of 15 of item A is $15x$. The cost of 10 of item B is $10y$. The cost of the A and B items together is $15x + 10y$. Since there are $15 + 10 = 25$ items, the average cost is $\frac{15x + 10y}{25}$.

12-F To factor $3x^2 - 33x + 90$, first factor out 3 to get $3(x^2 - 11x + 30)$. Finish factoring to get: $3(x - 6)(x - 5)$. Choice F has 2 of the factors.

13-E The area of a circle is πr^2. With the radius of $a - 3$, the area is $\pi(a - 3)^2 = \pi(a^2 - 6a + 9)$.

14-G The average of the two expressions will be their sum divided by 2.

$$\frac{(3a + 7) + (4a + 1)}{2}$$ Add $3a + 4a$ and $7 + 1$.

$$= \frac{7a + 8}{2}$$ Separate into two fractions.

$$= \frac{7a}{2} + \frac{8}{2}$$ Simplify $\frac{8}{2}$.

$$= \frac{7a}{2} + 4$$

15-E By definition, $\log_x 64$ is the power of x that it would take to be 64. That power is 3 from the right side of the equation. So, $x^3 = 64$. This equation is satisfied when $x = 4$.

16-F $-3x + 10 > 1$ The sum of -3 times x and 10 is greater than 1.

$-3x > -9$ Subtract 10.

$-3x > -9$ Divide by -3.

$x < 3$ Switch the inequality sign.

Mathematics Answer Review Workout D

17-C The problem tells you that $x = \frac{1}{2}y$ and that:

$$x + y = 44 \qquad \text{Substitute } \tfrac{1}{2}y \text{ for } x.$$

$$\tfrac{1}{2}y + y = 44 \qquad \text{Add.}$$

$$\tfrac{3}{2}y = 44 \qquad \text{Multiply both sides by } \tfrac{2}{3}.$$

$$y = \tfrac{88}{3}$$

$$x = \tfrac{1}{2}y = \tfrac{1}{2}\left(\tfrac{88}{3}\right) = \tfrac{44}{3}$$

The difference between x and y is $\tfrac{88}{3} - \tfrac{44}{3} = \tfrac{44}{3} = 14\tfrac{2}{3}$ miles.

18-K Obtuse angles measure between 90° and 180°. You need to decide which of the following is TRUE:

 I. Since the larger of $\angle A$ and $\angle B$ is less than 180°, and the smaller one is greater than 90°, their difference must be less than 90°. TRUE.

 II. Since both angles are greater than 90°, their sum is greater than 180°. The sum of the three angles of a triangle is equal to 180°. FALSE.

 III. Since both angles are less than 180°, their sum is less than 360°. The sum of the angles of a trapezoid is 360°, so they could be interior angles of a trapezoid. TRUE.

Note: By picking two angles slightly greater than 90° and trying to draw the 3 figures, then picking angles slightly less than 180° and trying to draw them again, you can probably decide how to ZAP this question.

19-B

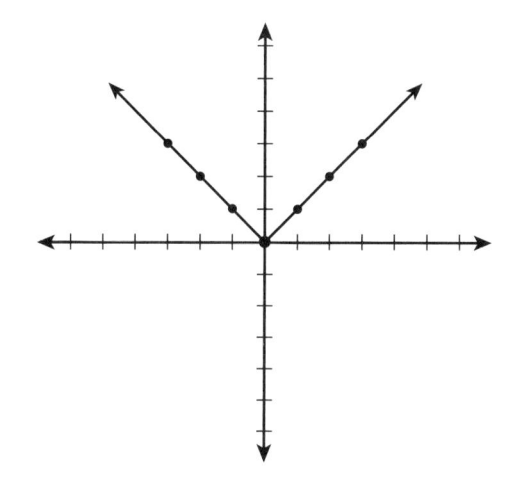

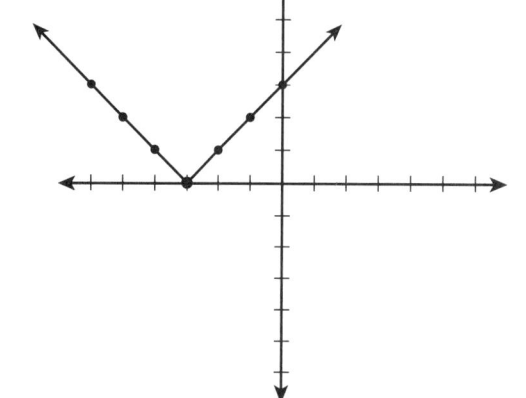

$y = |x|$

x	0	1	2	3	-1	-2	-3
y	0	1	2	3	1	2	3

$y = |x + 3|$

x	0	-1	-2	-3	-4	-5	-6
y	3	2	1	0	1	2	3

Therefore, graph of $y = |x + 3|$ is transformed 3 units to the left.

20-G The point where any line crosses the y-axis has an x-coordinate of zero. You can find the equation of the line and substitute $x = 0$ to find the y-coordinate of the point.

The slope is $\frac{4-1}{1-3} = \frac{3}{-2} = -\frac{3}{2}$.

Now put the slope and the point (1, 4) into point-slope form.

$y - y_1 = m(x - x_1)$

$y - 4 = -\frac{3}{2}(x - 1)$ Substitute $x = 0$.

$y - 4 = -\frac{3}{2}(0 - 1)$

$y - 4 = -\frac{3}{2}(-1)$

$y - 4 = \frac{3}{2}$

$y = 5\frac{1}{2}$

Note: Since the point must have an x-coordinate of zero, ZAP H, J, and K. If you think of going from B to A, you go up 3 and to the left 2. Since you only need to move 1 to the left to cross the y-axis, you only need to move up $\frac{1}{2}$ of 3, or $1\frac{1}{2}$, to reach the appropriate height. Point A is already up 4, so you would end up at $4 + 1\frac{1}{2} = 5\frac{1}{2}$.

Mathematics Answer Review Workout E

1-C The problem says that the total of the three days equals two-thirds of his acreage:

$$\frac{2}{3}(270) = 180$$

The amount for each of the three days is 40 for Monday, x for Tuesday, and $(40 + x) - 20$ or $x + 20$ for Wednesday.

$$40 + x + x + 20 = 180 \quad \text{Combine like terms.}$$
$$2x + 60 = 180$$

2-J The problem gives the side opposite $\angle A$ and asks for the hypotenuse. $\text{Sin } A = \frac{\text{side opposite}}{\text{hypotenuse}}$

$$0.500 = \frac{9}{AB} \quad \text{OR} \quad \overline{AB} = \frac{9}{0.500} = 18.00$$

Note: Since this is a 30°−60°−90° triangle, you can multiply the short leg by 2 to get the hypotenuse. $2(9) = 18$.

3-E In a square, a diagonal bisects the angles. Since $\overline{BD}$ is a diagonal of the square, $\angle CBE = 45°$. This means $\triangle BEC$ is a 45°−45°−90° triangle. The leg $\overline{EC}$ is the hypotenuse divided by $\sqrt{2}$.

$$\frac{4}{\sqrt{2}} = \frac{4\sqrt{2}}{2} = 2\sqrt{2}$$

Note: Or use the Pythagorean Theorem.

Let EC and $EB = x$

$$x^2 + x^2 = 4^2$$
$$2x^2 = 16$$
$$x^2 = 8$$
$$x = \sqrt{8}$$
$$x = \sqrt{4}\sqrt{2}$$

Therefore, $x = 2\sqrt{2}$

4-G Since the center of the circle is (0, 0) and the radius is 3, the equation of the circle is:

$$(x - 0)^2 + (y - 0)^2 = 9$$
$$x^2 + y^2 = 9 \quad \text{Divide each side by 9.}$$
$$\frac{x^2}{9} + \frac{y^2}{9} = 1$$

Note: For an equation to be a circle, the coefficients of the x^2 term and y^2 term must both be the same and positive when they are on the same side of the equation. You could ZAP J and K because they have no squared terms and F because the y^2 term is negative.

5-A Since the sum of the three angles must be 180°, we can use the known measures of 30° and 105° to infer that $m\angle B = 180 - 30 - 105 = 45°$. From there, we can use the law of sines:

$$\frac{30\sqrt{2}}{\sin(30°)} = \frac{b}{\sin(45°)}$$

Cross multiplying, we get:

$$(30\sqrt{2})\sin(45°) = b\sin(30°)$$

This is a good spot to use your calculator—just make sure it's in degree mode. Evaluating the left side, we get 30, and since $\sin(30°) = \frac{1}{2}$, the right side is $\frac{1}{2}b$. Thus:

$$30 = \frac{1}{2}b$$
$$b = 60$$

6-F The *y*-value of any point on the *x*-axis is zero.

7-B Numbers with negative exponents are the same as the reciprocal of the number with the positive exponent. Example: $x^{-\frac{1}{2}} = \frac{1}{x^{\frac{1}{2}}}$

$$4^{-\frac{3}{2}} = \frac{1}{4^{\frac{3}{2}}} = \frac{1}{\sqrt{4}^3} = \frac{1}{2^3} = \frac{1}{8}$$

8-J If two sides of the right triangle are the same length, then two angles are the same, and the other is 90°. That makes the triangle a 45°–45°–90° triangle. The hypotenuse is $\sqrt{2}$ times the length of a leg. $\sqrt{2}(\sqrt{5}) = \sqrt{10}$.

9-A Using the entries in the (1, 1) positions of the matrices (the 4, −3, and −9), we get the equation $4a - (-3) = -9$, which turns into $4a + 3 = -9$. Subtracting 3 from both sides gives $4a = -12$, so $a = -3$. Knowing that $a = -3$, we can solve for *x*, *y*, and *z* as follows:

$-3x - 7 = -22$, which gives us $x = 5$
$-3y - (-5) = 8$, or $-3y + 5 = 8$, which gives us $y = -1$
$-3z - 2 = -32$, which gives us $z = 10$.

With this in hand, $a\begin{bmatrix} x & x \\ y & y \end{bmatrix} = -3\begin{bmatrix} 5 & 5 \\ -1 & -1 \end{bmatrix} = \begin{bmatrix} -15 & -15 \\ 3 & 3 \end{bmatrix}$

(Note that in the work above, solving for *z* was actually unnecessary).

Mathematics Answer Review Workout E

10-F Since all of the equations are lines, there will not be a solution if the lines are parallel. If the lines are parallel, they have the same slope but the equations are not multiples of each other. If the equation of a line is written in the form of $y = mx + b$, then the slope is m. Write each equation in this form and see if the x coefficients are the same.

F. $y = \frac{3}{2}x + 2$

$y = \frac{3}{2}x + 7$

G. $y = -3x + 4$

$y = -\frac{3}{2}x + 4$

H. $y = \frac{3}{2}x + \frac{11}{2}$

$y = 3x + 7$

J. $y = 3x + 1$

$y = -3x + 1$

K. $y = -\frac{1}{3}x + \frac{2}{3}$

$y = -x + 1$

Since choice F is the only pair of equations with the same slope, then the lines in F are parallel, and the system has no solution.

11-B $\overline{AB}$ is the hypotenuse of the right triangle and $\overline{CB}$ is opposite the 40° angle and adjacent to the 50° angle. To find the length of $\overline{CB}$ you would need to use sin 40° or cos 50°. By looking at the choices, you can see that only one choice uses cos 50° and none of them use sin 40°. The actual equation would be $\cos 50° = \frac{\overline{CB}}{6}$ or $\overline{CB} = 6 \cos 50°$.

12-K Since the graph intersects the x-axis at $(-2, 0)$ and $(2, 0)$, the roots of the equation are 2 and -2. That means the equation in factored form is $y = (x - 2)(x + 2)$ or $y = x^2 - 4$. Another way to find the equation of the parabola is to use the form of a parabola $y = a(x - h)^2 + k$, where (h, k) is the vertex and a is some constant. Here the vertex is $(0, -4)$.

By substitution $y = a(x-0)^2 + (-4)$

$y = ax^2 - 4$

To find a, plug in any other point on the parabola. Substituting $(2, 0)$, you get

$0 = a(2)^2 - 4$

$0 = 4a - 4$

$4 = 4a$

$a = 1$

So the equation is $y = 1x^2 - 4$ or $y = x^2 - 4$.

Note: Since the parabola opens up instead of to the side, x will be squared in the equation and not y. So you can ZAP G and J.

13-C To see where the points are, make a coordinate axis and plot the points. Now you need to see if you can sketch each figure so that it intersects all 4 points. Each of them can be done except two perpendicular lines. Here are examples of the other 4 choices:

A.

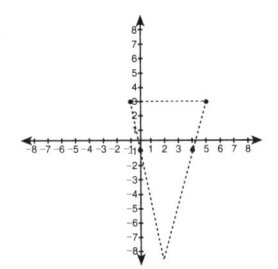

B.

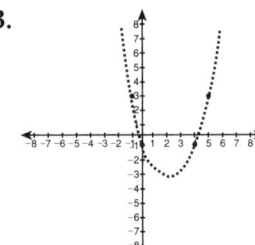

C.

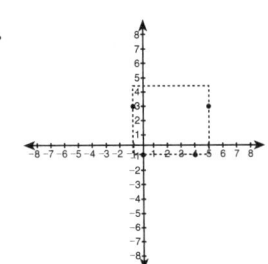

D.

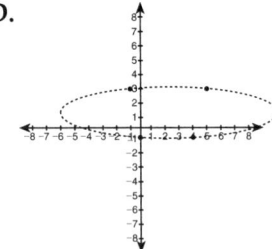

14-G Since the area of the square is 64, the length of a side is $\sqrt{64} = 8$. The area of $\triangle EBD$ is

$\frac{1}{2}$(base • height) $= \frac{1}{2}(8 • 8) = 32$. The area of $\triangle ABE$ equals the area of the square minus the areas

of $\triangle BCD$ and $\triangle EBD$. $64 - 20 - 32 = 12$

Mathematics Answer Review Workout E

15-E Since the first two points are on the same horizontal line, the length of that side of the triangle is the difference of the x-coordinates: $6 - 0 = 6$. Since the last two points are on the same vertical line, the length of that side is the difference of y-coordinates: $4 - 0 = 4$. Since the triangle is a right triangle, you can use the Pythagorean Theorem to find the length of the hypotenuse.

$$\sqrt{4^2 + 6^2} = \sqrt{16 + 36} = \sqrt{52}$$ The perimeter is the sum of all three sides.

$$4 + 6 + \sqrt{52} = 10 + \sqrt{52}$$

16-H To solve the inequality $|x - 6| > 3$, we need to solve two separate inequalities: $x - 6 > 3$, and $x - 6 < -3$. The first of these inequalities has a solution of $x > 9$, and the second has a solution of $x < 3$.

Note: Try $x = 0$. If it works, 0 must be in the solution. ZAP G, J, and K.

17-D Draw a coordinate axis and plot the points. The missing corner of the square is in the fourth quadrant. It has the same x-coordinate as $(1, 0)$ and the same y-coordinate as $(-2, -3)$.

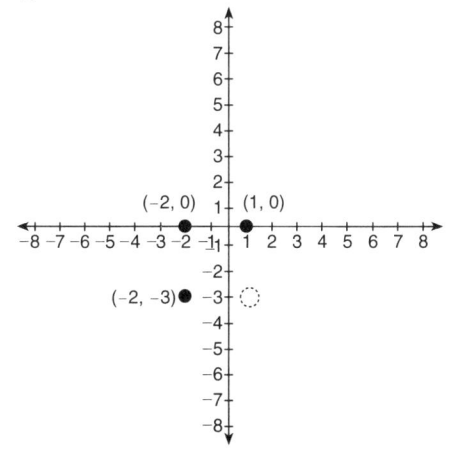

Note: If you realize that any pair of coordinates in the fourth quadrant will have a positive x-value and a negative y-value, you can ZAP all the other choices without figuring out the exact coordinates.

18-K $y = 2$ crosses the y-axis at $(0, 2)$. To find the distance between $(-1, -4)$ and $(0, 2)$, use the distance formula:

$$d = \sqrt{(x_2 - x_1)^2 + (y_2 - y_1)^2}$$

$$d = \sqrt{(0 - ^-1)^2 + (2 - ^-4)^2}$$

$$= \sqrt{(1)^2 + (6)^2}$$

$$= \sqrt{1 + 36}$$

$$= \sqrt{37}$$

19-D The factors are in the form of $(a - b)(a + b)$, so their product is $a^2 - b^2$ with $a = \sqrt{39}$ and $b = 2\sqrt{7}$.

$$(\sqrt{39} - 2\sqrt{7})(\sqrt{39} + 2\sqrt{7})$$
$$= (\sqrt{39})^2 - (2\sqrt{7})^2$$
$$= 39 - (4 \cdot 7)$$
$$= 39 - 28$$
$$= 11$$

Note: You could just foil the binomials to get the answer.

20-H The volume of the cube can be found by multiplying $10 \cdot 10 \cdot 10$. Using the formula $V = \pi r^2 h$, the volume of the cylinder is $\pi(4)^2 \cdot 9$. Therefore $10^3 - \pi(4)^2 \cdot 9$ is the required volume for answer H.

Mathematics Answer Review Workout F

1-A Since all of the heights in the problem are between 6 feet and 7 feet, average the inches and add the average to six feet. Let x be the number of inches for the fifth player. To find the average, add the inches for the 5 players and divide by 5. The problem says the average will equal 4.

$$\frac{1 + 2 + 3 + 5 + x}{5} = 4 \qquad \text{Add the numbers.}$$

$$\frac{11 + x}{5} = 4 \qquad \text{Multiply both sides of the equation by 5.}$$

$$11 + x = 20 \qquad \text{Subtract 11 from both sides.}$$

$$x = 9$$

The player would need to be 6'9''.

2-J Since $DECB$ has 2 parallel sides, it is a trapezoid. The formula for the area of a trapezoid is:

$$A = \tfrac{1}{2}(b_1 + b_2)h$$

$$\tfrac{1}{2}(4 + 5)(2) = 9$$

3-D The bread sells for $\tfrac{1}{2}$ of the regular price or $\tfrac{1}{2}(1.50) = 0.75$ or 75 cents. The tax is 4% of the sales price or $(.04)75 = 3$ cents. The cost, including tax, is $75 + 3 = 78$ cents.

Note: Once you figure out that the sale price is 75 cents, you know the total of the sales price and tax will be over 75 cents, so you can ZAP A, B, and C.

4-H Use the identity $\sin^2 x + \cos^2 x = 1$.

$$\sin^2 x + \left(\tfrac{1}{\sqrt{2}}\right)^2 = 1 \qquad \text{Square } \tfrac{1}{\sqrt{2}}.$$

$$\sin^2 x + \tfrac{1}{2} = 1 \qquad \text{Subtract } \tfrac{1}{2} \text{ from both sides.}$$

$$\sin^2 x = \tfrac{1}{2} \qquad \text{Take the square root of both sides.}$$

$$\sin x = \tfrac{1}{\sqrt{2}}$$

5-B Set up a proportion using the ratios of gallons to rooms with x as the missing amount.

$$\frac{3}{4} = \frac{\frac{1}{2}}{x}$$ Cross multiply.

$3x = 2$ Divide by 3.

$x = \frac{2}{3}$

6-G Break 96 into its prime factors.

$96 = 2 \cdot 48$
$ = 2 \cdot 2 \cdot 24$
$ = 2 \cdot 2 \cdot 2 \cdot 12$
$ = 2 \cdot 2 \cdot 2 \cdot 2 \cdot 6$
$ = 2 \cdot 2 \cdot 2 \cdot 2 \cdot 2 \cdot 3$

Since 2 and 3 are the only prime factors, G is the correct choice.

Note: If you look at the choices, you don't need to factor 96. You can ZAP F, H, and K because they are not prime. ZAP J because 19 is not a factor of 96. 3 is a prime number, and it divides into 96 without leaving a remainder, so it is a factor.

7-E

If the figure is symmetric about the dashed line, then the parts that correspond on the other side of the line are congruent. That means that the picture with all of the measurements on it looks like this. The perimeter is the distance around the figure or:

$4 + 2 + 2 + 4 + x + x = 12 + 2x.$

Mathematics Answer Review Workout F

8-J

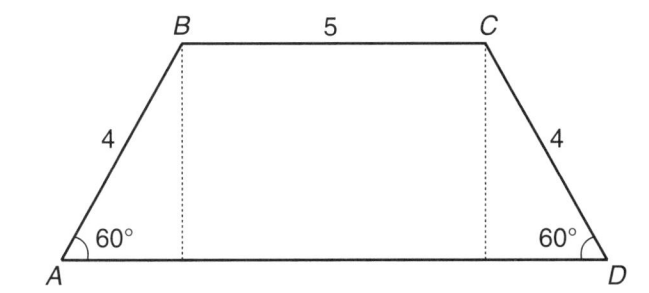

Since $ABCD$ is a trapezoid, $\overline{BC} \parallel \overline{AD}$. By the theorem that states, "If two parallel lines are cut by a transversal, then same-side interior angles are supplementary," the measure of $\angle A$ is $180° - 120° = 60°$. Since $\angle A = \angle D$, the trapezoid is isosceles and the measure of $\overline{CD}$ is 4. If you draw in the dotted lines, you get a rectangle and two $30°-60°-90°$ triangles. The short leg of each triangle is one half of the hypotenuse or $\frac{1}{2}(4) = 2$.

The length of $\overline{AD}$ is $2 + 5 + 2 = 9$.

9-C If one number is 3 and the other is x, then their product is $3x$, and their sum is $x + 3$. If their product is 5 greater than the sum, you need to add 5 to the sum to equal the product. The equation is $3x = (x + 3) + 5$.

10-K The $\csc \theta = \dfrac{1}{\sin \theta} = \dfrac{1}{\left(\frac{5}{13}\right)} = \dfrac{13}{5}$

11-B Because $\overline{SR} \parallel \overline{HJ}$, the measure of $\angle KSR$ is equal to the measure of $\angle KHJ$, and the measure of $\angle KRS$ is equal to the measure of $\angle KJH$ by the theorem that states, "If two parallel lines are cut by a transversal, then corresponding angles are congruent." That makes $\triangle KSR$ similar to $\triangle KHJ$ by the angle-angle similarity theorem. That means that the sides of the triangle form the proportion.

$$\dfrac{\overline{KR}}{\overline{KJ}} = \dfrac{\overline{SK}}{\overline{HK}}$$

If you let $= \overline{RJ} = x$, then the values to substitute into the proportion are:

$\overline{HK} = 6$, $\overline{KJ} = 4$, $\overline{SK} = \overline{HK} - \overline{HS} = 6 - 2 = 4$ and $\overline{KR} = \overline{KJ} - \overline{RJ} = 4 - x$.

$\dfrac{4-x}{4} = \dfrac{4}{6}$	Cross multiply.
$6(4 - x) = 4 \cdot 4$	Simplify.
$24 - 6x = 16$	Subtract 24 from each side.
$-6x = -8$	Divide each side by -6.
$x = \dfrac{8}{6} = \dfrac{4}{3}$	

12-G The cyclist traveled 45 miles in x hours, so her average speed was $\frac{45}{x}$. The problem says her average speed was $2x - 1$. So the equation to find x is:

$$\frac{45}{x} = 2x - 1 \qquad \text{Multiply by } x.$$

$$45 = 2x^2 - x \qquad \text{Subtract 45.}$$

$$2x^2 - x - 45 = 0 \qquad \text{Factor.}$$

$$(2x + 9)(x - 5) = 0 \qquad \text{Set each factor} = 0.$$

$$x = -\tfrac{9}{2} \quad \text{OR} \quad x = 5$$

Since x is the number of hours, x must be 5. Her speed is $2x - 1 = 2(5) - 1 = 9$ mph, so in 2 hours she traveled $9 \cdot 2 = 18$ miles.

13-E If a monomial has a variable, then it can only have positive integer powers of the variable. A has a negative power, B and C have fractional powers, and D is not a monomial because it is the sum of 2 monomials.

14-H $\left(a\sqrt{5}\right)^2$

$= a^2 \cdot 5$

$= 5a^2$

15-A The equation of line l is given in slope-intercept form. ($y = mx + b$ where m is the slope). The slope of $y = \tfrac{1}{2}x + 3$ is $\tfrac{1}{2}$. Put the slope and the point $(4, 3)$ of line p into point-slope form to find the equation of line p.

$$y - 3 = \tfrac{1}{2}(x - 4)$$

To find where it intersects the x-axis, set $y = 0$.

$$0 - 3 = \tfrac{1}{2}(x - 4) \qquad \text{Multiply both sides by 2.}$$

$$-6 = x - 4 \qquad \text{Add 4 to both sides.}$$

$$-2 = x$$

16-K $f(g(x)) = -\frac{3}{|x - 7|}$, which is defined for all real values of x unless $|x - 7| = 0$. The expression $|x - 7|$ is equal to 0 when and only when $x = 7$.

17-C If $\overline{BC}$ is the hypotenuse, then $\angle B$ is the other acute angle, not the right angle. The sum of the measures of the angles is 180°, so $\angle B = 180° - 90° - 35° = 55°$.

Mathematics Answer Review Workout F

18-F To find the intersection, use linear combination. Multiply the second equation by -2, and add it to the first to get an equation with x and no y in it.

$$\begin{cases} 4y + 3x = 8 \\ 2y - 7x = 4 \end{cases} \text{(Multiply by } -2\text{.)}$$

$$\begin{cases} 4y + 3x = 8 \\ -4y + 14x = -8 \end{cases}$$

$$\frac{17x}{17} = \frac{0}{17}$$

$$x = 0$$

Now plug 0 in for x in $4y + 3x = 8$.

$$4y + 3(0) = 8$$

$$4y = 8$$

$$y = 2$$

The point is (0, 2)

Note: You can find the right point by plugging the choices into the two equations. Remember, to be correct, the point must fit both equations.

19-D The height to the base of an isosceles triangle bisects the base (cuts it into two segments of 4 each). That means the height cuts the triangle into two right triangles with legs of 4 and 6. The hypotenuse can be found using the Pythagorean Theorem. The hypotenuse equals:

$$= \sqrt{4^2 + 6^2}$$

$$= \sqrt{16 + 36}$$

$$= \sqrt{52}$$

$$= \sqrt{4 \cdot 13}$$

$$= 2\sqrt{13}$$

The perimeter of the isosceles triangle is $2\sqrt{13} + 2\sqrt{13} + 8 = 8 + 4\sqrt{13}$.

20-F The cot A is the ratio of the side adjacent to A, which is 5, to the side opposite A, which is 7.

The cot $A = \frac{5}{7}$.

> You may encounter many defeats, but you must not be defeated. In fact, it may be necessary to encounter the defeats, so you can know who you are, what you can rise from, how you can still come out of it.
> —Maya Angelou

Reading Answer Review Workout A

1-A   The correct answer is A. A main idea is supported throughout a passage and not just in a few paragraphs. The passage builds to a point that is stated in the last paragraph—that Earth has a potent and vastly underrated capacity to keep itself healthy. The rest of the choices are too specific.

2-G   The correct answer is G. Lines 57–58 say "three and a half billion years ago, at the dawn of organic evolution . . ."

3-D   The correct answer is D. From lines 40–43, you can deduce that burning fossil fuels is a cause of increased levels of carbon dioxide. Before humans began burning fossil fuels, the concentration of carbon dioxide was two hundredths of a percent; now, after thousands of years of burning fossil fuels, the concentration is three hundredths of a percent.

4-H   The correct answer is H. The point of the paragraph is that no matter how substantial the abuse to this planet, Earth has the capacity to regenerate itself. A description of "moderate" toxic dumping does nothing to strengthen this argument. So you can ZAP F. The same is true of G and J. A description of a dumping that was "undeniably" toxic, however, would make sense in this context.

5-D   The correct answer is D. This question has a negative twist, asking which activity would Gaia *not* be responsible for. Answers A, B, and C are supported by the passage. See lines 50–52 (A), 53–54 (B), and 23 (C).

6-J   The correct answer is J. Lines 76–79 say that a nuclear war of major proportions would affect the participants but would not disturb Gaia. In other words, a nuclear war would destroy many forms of life, but it would not destroy the planet.

7-C   The correct answer is C. Lines 67–69 say that Gaia provides oxygen by splitting CO_2 during photosynthesis.

8-F   The correct answer is F. The author quotes Lovelock's proposal that Earth's components form "a complex system which can be seen as a single organism"; in other words, Earth is a living thing.

9-D   The correct answer is D. Lines 61 through 70 describe the process by which Gaia "has worked to keep the atmosphere pumped up richly with oxygen" and how she has accomplished this by "burying the carbon away in forms such as peat, coal, and oil."

10-F   The correct answer is F. Lines 17–18 mention that life created its physical environment.

11-C   The correct answer is C. Although Hannah is looking at a field that shows both the results of the recent harvest and the effects of the wheat trucks, she is not thinking about these things (A and D). Instead, she is thinking about the ranch when Selma moved there. (C): "*She wondered* what it must have been like when Selma . . ." The narrator also describes some of Hannah's childhood memories, but there is no indication that these memories are part of her current thoughts. In fact, we are specifically told that she is unable to remember the last time she had walked there. In the fiction passages on the ACT Reading Test, it is often necessary to recognize the narrator's voice and to understand what information comes from the narrator and what information comes from the narrator's knowledge of the characters' thoughts.

12-G   The correct answer is G. In paragraph 3 we are told that Hannah walked a little more than a mile to the top of a hill from which she could see the canyon nearby. The passage tells us that the ranch is half a day's ride from Alderdale (lines 14–15), so F can be ZAPPED. The river lies 30 miles from the canyon (line 29) so H can be ZAPPED. The bluffs (J) are next to the hill Hannah is standing on, so they can't be a half day's ride from the ranch; J can be ZAPPED.

13-C The correct answer is C. In lines 48–49, we are told, "This *wind* welcomed her, like she belonged here."

14-G The correct answer is G. The verb *slink* suggests creeping or crawling close to the ground. The narrator describes the canyon as "slinking through the hills." This figurative language creates an image of the canyon curving around the bases of a number of hills as it approaches the river, taking an indirect path because the hills are in the way. "Winding" (G) is the choice that best describes this. None of the other choices are suggested by the image.

15-B The correct answer is B. The question is difficult because you must understand the whole passage to understand Hannah's mood. The passage hints at a nostalgic tone throughout. In lines 15–18, Hannah reminisces about imagining the ranch house and yard as a ship. Paragraph 5 is primarily about her reminiscence of the land in general. In lines 37–40, she reminisces about being afraid of animals when she was younger, but the words, "She smiled" suggest that she is not afraid now—ZAP C. Nothing in the passage suggests that she is angry (A). Coot only comes along in the last two paragraphs; most of her walk is without him—ZAP D.

16-F The correct answer is F. Lines 41–49 mention the effect of the wind on Hannah. Not only does the wind remind Hannah of the feeling of being in the airplane, it also "grab[s] her by the shoulders, shake[s] her . . ." This is a strong effect. G cannot be correct, for line 48 says the wind "welcomed Hannah"; it didn't frighten her. H is incorrect because a comparison of the wind to an airplane has nothing to do with the old woman cited in line 51. J implies that Hannah's imagination is not to be trusted and that she "wildly exaggerates things." The tone of the passage suggests that although Hannah has a vivid imagination, she still has her senses about her.

17-A The correct answer is A. This question tests your ability to carefully read and interpret lines 50–54. The first sentence is a bit backwards: "She had learned to recognize *her* voice in these . . . winds"—who does *her* refer to? The next line tells you: "the voice of the old woman she imagined as the land" who, according to lines 53–55 is, "a combination of all the generations who had lived or wandered here." B is wrong because Selma is a real person (see line 12), not a voice in the wind. C is wrong because Hannah's family is not mentioned in relation to the wind. And D is wrong because "an old woman who once owned the land" suggests a real person, not an imaginary voice in the wind.

18-H The correct answer is H. As you read the passage, you need to understand what Hannah is doing and why she is doing it. Hannah behaves as someone would who has grown up there and has been away for several years. Lines 15–16 give the best clue: "When Hannah was growing up . . ." and go on to mention how she imagined the ranch back then. Again in lines 37–38 we get a clue that Hannah grew up on the ranch: "She smiled, remembering when she used to be afraid of the coyotes and bobcats." And we know that although Hannah has been away, she refers to the ranch house as home (line 69). F is wrong because no mention is made of Hannah's staying with Selma. G is wrong because the passage never says that Hannah has moved back to the ranch. J is wrong because the passage doesn't mention that she spent only her summers at the ranch.

19-B The correct answer is B. This question asks you to picture a simile. Hannah imagined that the ranch house and its yard was a ship "floating through the brown-yellow [wheat] fields" (lines 17–18). If the house is a ship, then the field is water. A is *not* correct because Hannah included the green grass surrounding the house as part of the ship (line 16).

20-J The correct answer is J. This question has a negative twist because it asks which statement is *not* supported. Although Hannah decides to return to the ranch (in the last paragraph), nothing says she really wants to be with the people there, so J is *not* supported. Answer F is supported in lines 25–26: "Whenever she remembered the ranch, this [the canyon] was the place she thought of." G is supported. The tone of the whole passage suggests that Hannah feels close to the land; we don't know if she feels that close to the people. And Coot, the dog, did startle her (H).

Reading Answer Review
Workout B

1-A The correct answer is A. Lines 17–18 contain the topic sentence of the paragraph, which says "the acquisition of language by children may offer insights into the origins of speech." Choices B and D are very *ZAP*-able because they are false statements.

2-F The correct answer is F. Lines 43–48 say that children understand basic grammar and can combine the meaning of several words into one word when they say things like "out" and "bottle." These are the symbolic combinations referred to in F. Choices G, H, and J exploit a potential misunderstanding of what the passage says about grammar.

3-D The correct answer is D. "Mutually unintelligible languages" is contrasted with "same brain-generated language" in lines 68–69. The word "Instead" in line 70 sets up this contrast, suggesting that mutually unintelligible languages have few words that can be understood by speakers of different languages.

4-J The correct answer is J. Lines 34–36 say, "The child's acquisition of the structure and meaning of language has been called the most difficult intellectual achievement in life." However, it is noted in the next sentence that most children master it easily.

5-C The correct answer is C. The paragraph implies that our current system of communication is not merely a call system in which an individual sound has a distinct meaning. Lines 6 through 9 say that the call system eventually became a system based on small units of sound that could be put together in different ways to form meanings. It's reasonable to infer that a call, which is not directly defined in the paragraph, is a single unit of sound with a specific meaning.

6-J The correct answer is J. This question has a negative twist, asking for the choice *not* supported by the last paragraph. F is *stated* in lines 65–66 ("Whether this device in fact exists is not yet clear."). G is *stated* in lines 59–62 ("to explain the child's early acquisition and creative use of grammatical structure. . . . One set of theoreticians of grammar suggests that there may be a language acquisition device"). H is *implied* in lines 63–65 ("As the forebrain evolved, this language acquisition device may have become part of our biological inheritance.") For J to be true, this device must exist. However, it is only theoretical at this point.

7-C The correct answer is C. An open language is defined in lines 1–3: utterances combined in various ways to produce new meanings. Items **I** and **II** combine words to create meanings that are *not* represented by just one word.

8-G The correct answer is G. To paraphrase lines 15–18, human adults changed their form of communication from calls to open language in a millennia; children change from using calls as infants to using open language in three to four years. Speaking children are compared to call-using adults.

9-B The correct answer is B. The question asks for a skill that humans are naturally equipped for but must learn. When born, humans cannot walk but soon learn to do so as their legs and sense of balance develop naturally. Hearing normally doesn't require learning (A). Reading and writing are not natural, for some cultures do not have a written language (C and D).

10-H The correct answer is H. The passage doesn't use any one culture, race, or language as an example, but speaks of human language acquisition in general terms. Thus, the passage implies that language acquisition is universal.

11-D The correct answer is D. The "habit-forming programmes" are mentioned in lines 11–12, but it isn't until lines 18–22 that the author implies a connection between habit-forming television shows and the mass audience that watches for the sake of watching anything. The words "that they are there" (lines 21–22) suggest watching from habit, a characteristic of a mass audience.

12-G The correct answer is G. The main idea can be stated in many places in a passage, but it must be supported by the whole passage. Choice G is first suggested in lines 13–15: "But, of course . . . a declining audience need not also mean a less enthusiastic one." Then, lines 32–35 ("there has never been a larger . . . public for the kind of film which only a few years ago would have seemed desperately specialized") also suggest that the correct answer is G. The first paragraph begins by talking about the different names for cinema, but the issue is quickly dropped (F). Hollywood empires declined, but the passage does not state that this created serious economic problems for film producers (H). Answer J is too specific; a generation having a vocabulary of the screen is only a small detail from the passage.

13-A The correct answer is A. Throughout the passage, the author uses the term "cinema" for *all* the things mentioned in A. B, C, and D are too specific. In line 24, "cinema" means a mass-market motion picture (D); in lines 36 and 51, it means an experimental film (C); and in line 71, it refers to European films (B).

14-H The correct answer is H. Paragraph 3 talks about how filmmaking is influenced by trends of the day. Film magazines uncover new trends and raise the viewing audience's expectations. If a director fails to fulfill a prediction set forth by these trends, that director would seem to be betraying a promise created by fashions in the media. F, G, and J are not suggested by the passage.

15-B The correct answer is B. Questions such as this ask the reader to recognize what is meant by a statement in the passage. The statement is explained in the rest of the paragraph, where the reader is told that too often the public pays more attention to film fashions than to the movie (B). Choices A, C, and D contain statements that go beyond what is said in the third paragraph.

16-G The correct answer is G. Lines 79–81 describe how the studios could support a young artist like Orson Welles: "A studio could take the time to let young artists and actors develop, sure that it would still be there when the time came round to get the best out of them." Lines 81–83 describe the support he received: He was allowed to study films for the better part of a year before directing *Citizen Kane.* F, H, and J are not mentioned by the author in connection with Welles.

17-D The correct answer is D. An indication that a more receptive audience had evolved is found in lines 30–35 and throughout the passage. The other choices either disagree with the passage or are not supported by it. The growth of large film studios (A) was connected to mass-market films. Publicity about new directors (B) and specialization of film magazines (C) are treated more as potentially harmful results than causes of specialized film production.

18-F The correct answer is F. Lines 17–22 tell us that a large number of people may watch the same programs just to be watching *something*. Quality isn't always an issue. Choices G and H are directly contradictory to the information in lines 13–17. Use the true/false strategy to ZAP J because of the word "always."

19-C The correct answer is C. Lines 15–17 say: "The *Pilkington Report,* in another context, has nailed the fallacy of claiming to gauge public taste on a purely statistical basis." There is no evidence that the report discussed either movies or television A, B, and D. It is clear that the report pointed out the shortcomings of relating statistical evidence to matters of taste.

20-F The correct answer is F. Overall, the author had positive and negative things to say about the evolution of cinema. After speaking of "heavy casualties" in line 73, she describes how the large studio system could afford to let an artist develop, but that "this could hardly happen now" (lines 83–84). When you see these different viewpoints, you can conclude that the author has mixed feelings about the change in cinema over the years.

Reading Answer Review
Workout C

1-D The correct answer is D. The first two paragraphs introduce the reader to the town, Miss Emily, her house, and her death. The remaining four paragraphs describe an incident that occurred as a result of Miss Emily's refusal to pay taxes.

2-F The correct answer is F. Lines 27–30 say, "Colonel Sartoris invented an involved tale to the effect that Miss Emily's father had loaned money to the town, which the town . . . preferred this way of repaying."

3-A The correct answer is A. The answer is in the second paragraph, which begins by saying the house had once been located on the town's "most select street," and then describes the gradual decay of that neighborhood.

4-H The correct answer is H. A clue to the meaning of "archaic" can be found in the character of Miss Emily. She is a recluse in an ancient house. She refuses to keep up with the times. It would be consistent with all we know about her for her choice of writing paper to be old-fashioned.

5-B The correct answer is B. You know Miss Emily would not have asked for assistance (lines 26–27), so you can ZAP A. It says that Colonel Sartoris made up the story about Miss Emily's father lending money to the town, so you can ZAP C. There is no evidence that the town wants to preserve her house, so you can ZAP D. It is reasonable to infer, however, that Colonel Sartoris and the townspeople valued her. B is the correct choice.

6-H The correct answer is H. The question asks how we, the readers, know that the whole town thinks Miss Emily was an eccentric. The only clue we have is that the whole town went to her funeral and that the women were curious because no one but her servant had entered her home "in at least ten years." The rest of the choices do not demonstrate that the townspeople found her eccentric, only that she was eccentric.

7-D The correct answer is D. In fiction, a person's character is often revealed in the way that person behaves and the way he or she relates to others. Physical appearance is important, but not as important as descriptions that show how a character behaves and thinks, and what others think of that character. A hints at what the town thinks of her. B and C show her actions. Her physical appearance (D) does the least to tell the reader who Miss Emily was.

8-J The correct answer is J. The entire story proceeds from the time in 1894 (described in paragraph 3) when Colonel Sartoris declared that taxes on Miss Emily's father's property would be remitted (canceled) in perpetuity. Although the first paragraph of the story mentions that the people of Jefferson wanted to see Miss Emily's house, that (choice H) is not the first event in the sequence of events the story describes. The visit from the town board (choice G) happens because the board wants Miss Emily to begin paying the taxes that she claims Colonel Sartoris excused. The supposed loan of money to the town by Miss Emily's father is described in line 27 as a "tale," so choice F is not a true statement and can be ZAPPED.

9-B The correct answer is B. If the later generation had accepted that Colonel Sartoris had the right to exempt Miss Emily from the town laws, the town officials never would have visited her. Choice A is unlikely because nothing in the passage suggests that the new town officials wouldn't support poor individuals. C is not correct, because they were being respectful of Miss Emily by writing to her and offering to give her a ride to the sheriff's office. D is not mentioned at all in the passage.

10-F The correct answer is F. The pronoun "our" indicates that Jefferson "belongs" to the narrator. In other words, the narrator lives there.

11-B The correct answer is B. The passage frequently touches upon how public and social "goods" are not frequently considered by economic theory and implies that the reader should consider how this omission has negative results. Although the author mentions some of what he learned in college (A), including "the art of assessing investment options to maximize financial return" (B), neither describes the main aim of the passage. The destructive results of speculation and fraud (D) represent a detail in support of the author's primary purpose.

12-H The correct answer is H. In paragraph 3, the author says, "money is only an accounting chit with no intrinsic existence or value outside the human mind." Later, in paragraph 5, he expands on this idea: "It is easy to confuse money with the real wealth for which it can be exchanged—our labor, ideas, land, gold, health care, food, and all the other things with value in their own right. The illusions of phantom wealth are so convincing that most Wall Street players believe the wealth they are creating is real." In other words, money has no *essential* or inherent value other than the value we attach to it in our minds. Money is a construct.

13-C The correct answer is C. The term *phantom wealth* appears in paragraphs focused on investment in the stock market (paragraphs 1 and 5). Money that was made producing a social good (B) would be real wealth, the opposite of phantom wealth. Printing more bills (A) would be a close guess, if you hadn't read the passage, which does not discuss this part of the economic system.

14-J The correct answer is J. The author makes the point that utility simply measures the amount of stuff bought and earned, i.e., a person's affluence (J). "Usefulness" (H) is one common synonym of utility, but in this case, it does not apply. That kind of system might seem to ignore the neediness (F) of others, but this concept is tangential to the overall equation of utility with wealth.

15-A The correct answer is A. As one of its primary rhetorical strategies, this passage uses the example of the rural mountain village in the Phillipines (last two paragraphs). The passage does not use any quotations (B), metaphors (C) or allegories (D).

16-J The correct answer is J. Answer J ("Money can't buy happiness.") best reflects the inequality of money and happiness (or satisfaction), which is central to the author's revision of the utility theory. Answers G and H discuss money management, which is not really the topic of this passage. Answer F reflects the illusory nature of money, but is often used as an encouragement to spend.

17-A The correct answer is A. Financial poverty can coexist with important social wealth. The notion that a simple life is happier than one of wealth and possessions (C) is a simplification of the author's meaning. A simple life can be happier, but it is not always. And the author would disagree that happiness cannot be analyzed (B); he cites the efforts of one researcher, Max-Neef, to do so. The diversity of incomes (D) is not an issue in the passage. Rather, the author describes the social "wealths" or assets of neighborliness, belonging, safety, trust, and social cohesion coexisting with financial poverty (A).

18-G The correct answer is G. Both authors contend that conventional or "orthodox" economics fails to measure much of what is really of value, such as the social good, or social wealth. This discussion of the shortcomings of economics is not framed as a question of its "scientific" (A) aspirations. The alternative theories don't need to be taught to everyone (J); for instance the author of Passage B is not suggesting that the Filipino villagers he describes should study Max-Neef. The difference between needs and wants (H) is mentioned by Passage A but not Passage B.

19-C The correct answer is C. Passage A focuses on money earned while Passage B focuses mainly on money spent. Passage A is preoccupied with the definition of wealth insofar as it is earned, whether by means useful to society, not useful to society, or out of "thin air." Passage B looks at the "utility" of that wealth mainly in terms of consumption of goods to meet needs and wants. Passage A does focus on defining wealth (A), but Passage B, while it mentions poverty, is not focused on *defining* poverty. The terms *phantom wealth* and *real wealth* (B) are only present in Passage A, not Passage B. Finally, neither passage focuses much on practical economics (D); they are mostly working with theory.

20-G The correct answer is G. The author of Passage A describes his time in graduate school as a way into the topic of economics. The author of Passage B uses the first-person pronouns, "we," "us," and "our." ZAP F. Passage B cites expert opinion (G), but Passage A does not. Both passages use rhetorical questions (H). Both passages use comparison and contrast (J), whether between real and phantom wealth in Passage A or between the United States and the Philippines village in Passage B.

Reading Answer Review Workout D

1-C The correct answer is C. Lines 66–68 say: "*Noh's* appeal is limited, since its form was fixed long ago. The language, based on aristocratic speech of the fourteenth century, is unintelligible to most people today."

2-H The correct answer is H. Lines 3–5 say: "When Buddhism was introduced into Japan during the sixth century A.D., dance plays set to music came with it."

3-A The correct answer is A. Lines 11–15 say that both *dengaku* and *sarugaku* "were medleys of disconnected songs, dances, and short sketches." Short sketches are considered theater.

4-G The correct answer is G. The sentence says the majority of lines were sung or intoned, and few were spoken. From this sentence you can deduce that the meaning of "intoned" is similar to "sung." Of the choices, chanting is most similar to singing.

5-D The correct answer is D. In lines 35–40, the author describes a highly structured social system. In lines 31–32, the author mentions that the arts were "flourishing"; in lines 47–49 he says that forms were being created "that are still considered the high point in Japanese artistic expression. There is no evidence in the passage for choice A; choice B is true but it's not the main idea; choice C is a detail from the passage.

6-F The correct answer is F. Lines 13–14 say that *sarugaku* grew out of ritualistic elements imported from China, and lines 15–17 say that *Noh* evolved out of *sarugaku*. Thus, Noh developed from ritual entertainments that came from China, and lines 3–5 suggest that these entertainments were influenced by Buddhism.

7-A The correct answer is A. Lines 5–9 say that the right to perform *bugaku* is passed down through generations of families with hereditary rights to the art form.

8-H The correct answer is H. Lines 19–20 say: "*Noh* reached its highest point with Kannami's son, Zeami Motokiyo (1363–1443)." The fourteenth and fifteenth centuries are the years following 1300 and 1400.

9-B The correct answer is B. Lines 66–67 say that *Noh*'s form "was fixed long ago." You can ZAP A because Japanese theater flourished during the period of the shogunate. You can ZAP C because there is no evidence that Zeami's innovations caused *Noh* plays to gain acceptance. You can ZAP D because lines 68–69 say that *Noh*'s language is "unintelligible to most persons today." That leaves B.

10-G The correct answer is G. Lines 50–56 talk about Buddhist influence on *Noh*. They say that Zeami adopted the conviction that beauty lies in suggestion, simplicity, subtlety, and restraint.

11-C The correct answer is C. C is a recurring theme in each of the five paragraphs. The other choices are too specific to be the main topic. The first paragraph talks about how stars "burn" (A), but then explains the role of gravity. The force that binds atoms (B) is discussed only in the first paragraph, and how gas clouds are formed (D) is discussed only in the second paragraph.

12-G The correct answer is G. It is important to note that this question is asking for the *second* most common element, which is helium (lines 53–54).

13-A The correct answer is A. Lines 69–72 say that the shrinking of a gas cloud is referred to as "a collapse." The word *collapse* implies that the contraction is sudden and rapid.

14-J The correct answer is J. The context of lines 11–15 compares "profound" to "superficial." *Superficial* refers to chemical reactions that do not alter the basic nature of the atom. When nuclear reactions are said to be *profound*, it means that they alter the basic nature of the atom.

15-D The correct answer is D. The first sentence states "a star burns only in the sense that it . . . gives off light somewhat the way a flame of a match . . . gives off light." The rest of the paragraph contrasts a candle's flame to a star's release of energy.

16-F The correct answer is F. The passage explains that stars are formed when gravity pulls the particles in gas clouds together. Thus, all stars began as gas clouds.

17-B The correct answer is B. This question has a negative twist, asking which would *not* result in a gas cloud's forming into a star. Lines 61–62 say that if the particles of a gas cloud are "moving fast enough, they may disperse before they can fall together."

18-J The correct answer is J. The paragraph repeatedly touches on the difference between nuclear and chemical reactions. Choice F is not stated in the passage; G is true, but only in normal chemical reactions and not in the nuclear reactions that create stars. Choice H is unclear. Atoms combine into molecules in normal chemical reactions, but star formation is a nuclear reaction, which is far more complex.

19-B The correct answer is B. Lines 38–39 say, "Isaac Newton first recognized the existence of this force." The only "force" described in the preceding passage (lines 22–27) is gravity (lines 24–25). Occasionally, outside knowledge you possess from other courses may help you answer test questions, although don't expect it to happen very often. If you have previously learned about Newton's experiments with gravity in science courses, this question will be easier.

20-H The correct answer is H. Lines 19–20 say "a star's heat comes from nuclear reactions"—or the nuclei of atoms hitting each other. A nuclear reactor also creates heat through the collisions of subatomic particles.

Reading Answer Review
Workout E

1-A The correct answer is A. Each of the four choices suggests troubled family relations and is found in the passage. The mention of divorce (line 6) comes first, followed by D (lines 16–20), B (lines 32 and 35), and C (line 36).

2-F The correct answer is F. Line 1 says, "My father stands in the kitchen . . ." and line 7 says, "I stand in the doorway, watching him do dishes." Al doesn't enter the kitchen until after the conversation begins.

3-B The correct answer is B. Lines 16–17 say, "For the last several years, I have felt peculiar around my father . . . ."

4-J The correct answer is J. The clue to the meaning of "derisive" is Al's attitude throughout the passage. Al is trying to make his father believe that he doesn't care about his opinion or the track team. Under these circumstances, he would most likely try to make his laugh sound mocking.

5-A The correct answer is A. This question asks for a probable reason, so you need to see which answer is likely and compare it to those that are definitely not supported by the passage. We know that Al seems to be unhappy, and he is annoyed by the coach's efforts to recruit him, so it is likely that he wants to avoid group activities (A). There is no evidence that he quarreled with other runners (B). He doesn't mention that he wants to spend more time with his father or join the team (C). Since the coach has apparently seen him running, there is no reason to assume he dislikes it (D).

6-H The correct answer is H. Al reflects three times on the trouble he has communicating with his father: lines 18–19 ("I don't like to be alone with him. I don't know what to say"); lines 72–73 ("Sometimes I think I'd like him better if we did yell at each other"); and lines 75–76 ("I stop, look at the floor. Perhaps my voice is too sharp, full of the same bitterness as his"). None of the other choices are supported by the passage.

Reading Answer Review Workout E

7-B   The correct answer is B. The frustration of Al's father is suggested in lines 57–59, when he says, "Would it compromise you that much to join something, once in your life?"

8-F   The correct answer is F. Line 36 ("Sometimes I hate my father for his sarcasm") refers to his remark, "One of your pals from school," in line 32. There is no evidence that the other choices are sarcastic.

9-C   The correct answer is C. Al compares his face to his parents' faces in lines 48–50. The words "strong," "cold," and "arrogant" do more than describe a face; they describe the person behind the face.

10-G   The correct answer is G. Once Al discovers that his father has spoken with the coach, he becomes resentful and withdrawn. In lines 38–39, he does not answer his father immediately, and in line 44 he refers to the coach's remarks as "crap."

11-A   The correct answer is A. Lines 44–45 say, "it was generally the idea or concept of the animal which the artist expressed." B is not true because lines 64–66 imply that the carvings could be very realistic. There is no evidence that the artists had to obey any religious rules (C). D is not true because lines 29–30 say that the relationship between man and certain animals was intimate.

12-H   The correct answer is H. Lines 14–15 suggest that a Northwest Coast object is easily recognized. Lines 17–19 explain that established designs are repeated over and over. These established designs, which are later described as the heritage of the culture, are what make Northwest Coast Indian art easy to recognize.

13-D   The correct answer is D. Lines 9–12 say: "Even when his products were made to serve practical purposes the shapes and decorations were devised to have meaning; and even further, a meaning that would enhance the use of the product."

14-G   The correct answer is G. Line 41 describes "the line of demarcation" between men and animals as being "slight." Since the passage suggests many times the strong connection between humans and animals, it makes sense that the line of "separation" is slight.

15-C   The correct answer is C. Lines 24–27 say: "The world was seen by the Northwest Coast Indian as the habitation of a multiplicity of spirits in which the human spirit slips almost imperceptibly into those of various animals, and vice versa."

16-J   The correct answer is J. Line 66 suggests that the eyes give the carving a sense of having inner life.

17-B   The correct answer is B. One way to solve this type of problem is to check each foil and ZAP those that seem most clearly "suggested" by the passage. Choice A is strongly supported. ZAP it. Choice B is questionable—leave it. Choice C is somewhat difficult because the passage doesn't state directly that the animals were well known. However since the animals are beavers, whales, etc., there is the "suggestion" that they are well known. ZAP C. Now the choice is between B and D. There seems to be more support in the passage for D than B, so B is the answer.

18-H   The correct answer is H. This question has a negative twist, asking which item is *least* likely to be a Northwest Coast Indian artifact. The art of the Northwest Coast Indian emphasized animal and human features represented either as symbols or realistic figures. H is the only choice that omits the human or animal element.

19-D   The correct answer is D. Lines 74–76 say that the identities of the figures in a piece of art may have been known only to the man for whom it was made and the man who made it.

20-J   The correct answer is J. This question asks you to infer something that is *not* stated but is implied in the passage. F is wrong; while the author does try demonstrate the depth of meaning behind the art, he is not saying that it is the most beautiful Native American art. G is wrong, because the author does not imply that the Northwest Coast Indians were closer to nature than other Native American cultures. H is wrong, because the passage only discusses the art of the Northwest Coast Indians. J is the only reasonable inference you can make.

Reading Answer Review
Workout F

1-C   The correct answer is C. The passage is centrally concerned with the use of poetry in advertising. Poetry is an art form, and advertising is used to sell products. The author indicates that the ads diminish poetry. She is not concerned with the popularity of a particular type of product (A); she mentions knits but no specific item made of knits. Although poetry is defined (B) within the passage (for instance, in the quote from Aristotle), the overall purpose of the passage is not to define poetry but to explore the meanings of its use in advertisements. Product design (D) is not discussed in the passage.

2-J   The correct answer is J. There are two definitions of *knit*: 1) to make a garment or blanket with interlocking loops of yarn; 2) to unite or cause to unite. In using the metaphor, "a poem ought to be well-knit," the author is comparing a poem to a knitted object. Like a well-knitted object, a good poem should be unified; its parts should be well connected. Poems don't have to rhyme (F). Metaphors have no obvious connection to knit products (G, H), though the author uses a metaphor to connect poetry to knitting.

3-B   The correct answer is B. The quotation marks around the phrase, "Introspection comes naturally in the warmth of a relaxed ribbed sweater" clearly indicate that the author is referring to text that has been printed in the magazine. The concepts of "a reproduction" (A), an "imitation" (C), and something worth mentioning in the news (D) can be meanings of the word *copy* but are not supported by the context of the passage.

4-F   The correct answer is F. The sentences in the passage focus on a poet's recognizable style; i.e., the poet doesn't sound like everyone else. Although there can be musicality in some poetry, the article isn't referring to any musical tones (G). While a poet's vocabulary (H) is an element that makes up voice (style), vocabulary alone does not create the poet's voice. While productivity (J) can be important to a writer's success, it is not the main focus of the opening sentences of this passage, which is the recognizable style of the writing, not how much writing the poet is churning out.

5-B   The correct answer is B. The adverb *stupidly* (line 69) certainly helps with this item. The author is making fun of her own need to appear intelligent, to enhance "whatever intellectual qualities [she] may possess." There is nothing sentimental (A) about these sentences. There is satire (C); however, it is not political satire. Her satire has more to do with her own uncommon feelings about Polartec. Finally, there is no apparent exaggeration (D), or overstatement, in this description.

6-F   The correct answer is F. The "proliferation of choice" is identified as a cause of the situation the author describes—having one's "outward appearance . . . interpreted by the public as a decision" (F)—but the author is not arguing that people have too many choices (G). The author concedes that "you may not have a choice" (H), but this is just one condition that is discussed, not the focus. "Style" (J) is central in this discussion, but generic style (the dictates of fashion) are not as important as personal style.

7-C   The correct answer is C. The author moves abruptly from big-picture ideas (political implications worthy of political analysis) to a more pedestrian topic: Polartec. No comparison is being made with a simile (A), nor is an exaggeration being made through hyperbole (B). The transition leads to the main topic of the passage, not a slight digression (D).

Reading Answer Review Workout F

8-J The correct answer is J. The author consistently draws parallels between poetry and consumer culture (J) in both passages. Leisure time (F) is briefly mentioned in Passage A but not in Passage B. Passage A is more concerned with the advertising of products, particularly clothes, than with who wears them (G); Passage B briefly discusses clothing choices but does not limit that to women. The poet's role in an industrialized society (H) is not discussed in either passage.

9-C The correct answer is C. The author inserts herself into the text, whether by describing how she has been collecting examples of ads that feature "poetry" or by confessing her attraction to Polartec. The passages spend little or no time discussing other poets' techniques (A) or defining literary terminology (B). While she asks questions of the audience (D) in Passage 1, the questions she asks in Passage 2 are to represent the questions a new poet might ask him- or herself.

10-G The correct answer is G. The author's approach to her subject is experimental in that she says she learned "how to think and talk about poetry in ways that are my own." She is not being "reverent" (F) about her subject matter; in fact, she pokes fun at herself. She contradicts herself (for instance, on the topic of poetry and knits) and she makes abrupt transitions, such as the transition to the discussion of Polartec. She does all of these things deliberately and decisively, not "tentatively" (H). Nothing about her work is "sensationalist" (J).

11-B The correct answer is B. Although germs are extremely small (A), the "catalogue" refers to data *about* the germs, not the germs themselves. Catalogues often divide items into subcategories (C), but the focus of the discussion is on the number of items listed (10,000) not on their sub-classification. The sentence begins, "Beyond the fact that they don't play by the rules of taxonomy that are used to shoehorn animals and plants into groups...". This means that the author is excluding the lack of evidence for discrete species (D) from the subsequent discussion.

12-H The correct answer is H. Eukaryotes are defined (F), but this is not the focus. The difference between plants and animals (G) is not discussed. The notion of biologists being happy or "content" is part of the discussion early in the paragraph, but the reason for this contentment is different from that cited in (J). This paragraph essentially builds toward the last sentence, which becomes the pivotal idea of the entire passage.

13-D The correct answer is D. Although an archaic term, "animalcules" is the only one that fits. Protists (A), Eukaryotes (B) and Prokaryotes (C) are identified as subcategories of the "miniature organisms" or microbes (see lines 14–18, "The prevailing scheme . . . archaea").

14-F The correct answer is F. The author uses the word *extremist* (G) in line 94, but in a completely different context, speaking not of views or people who hold those views, but about species and their sizes and habitats. The author is not arguing for evolution (H); he simply assumes it. The author does not explore the similarities of diverse species (J); rather, he focuses on how limited our knowledge is because we do not live in water, and we are so relatively large compared to the majority of species.

15-A The correct answer is A. The point of the gigantism (B) the author discusses is that we humans are gigantic compared to the majority of species. Hostile organisms (C), while the standard fare of nightmares and sci-fi films, are not discussed in this passage. Sensations are the raw data of empiricism, but the extremity (D) that is mentioned in the passage refers to our place in the animal kingdom. Rather, the empiricist's nightmare is that the data provided by our senses are inadequate for understanding our world, and this is the author's main point.

16-G The correct answer is G. If you read the topic sentences of the two subsequent paragraphs, you see, first, "The first cause of our estrangement is our size," then "Our living on land further distances us. . . ." From this pattern, we can see that "estrangement" is a kind of distancing, or separation. Emotions such as contempt (F) and conditions such as disturbance (J) play no role in the passage. The issue in not familiarity (H) but a lack of familiarity.

17-A The correct answer is A. This is a straightforward item. Most creatures are small and live in wet environments. Humans are comparatively large and live on land.

18-J The correct answer is J. Passage A describes the "brilliant application of the microscope by Robert Hooke and Antonie van Leeuwenhoek," and Passage B states, "Only when we mastered glass and were able to produce clear, polished lenses were we able to gaze through a microscope," and so on. DNA sequencing (F) is discussed in neither passage. The fact that few microscopic species have been catalogued (G) and the difference between prokaryotes and eukaryotes (H) are each discussed only in Passage A.

19-D The correct answer is D. Both authors emphasize that science still has a long way to go in understanding microbes. *Disdain* (A) is too strong a word for their attitudes toward the profession they themselves are part of. Passage A stops short of support (B) for the methods of taxonomy. There is no discussion of a central theory (C).

20-H The correct answer is H. Passage B begins and ends with a discussion of the animal kingdom. While it does mention bacteria, which are not strictly part of the animal kingdom, it remains mainly focused on the animal kingdom. Passage A spends considerable space on other kingdoms: fungi, protists, bacteria, and archaea. Eukaryotes (F) are discussed in Passage A, not Passage B. Vertebrates (G) and organisms visible to the naked eye (J) are the main focus of the biologists that Passage B describes, but not the main focus of the passage itself.

> What you get by achieving your goals is not as important as what you become by achieving your goals.
> —Henry David Thoreau

Science Answer Review Workout A

Passage I (Research Summaries)

1-C The passage explains that pumps are in both systems, so D can be eliminated. You can figure out that a heater is required because if System 1 loses heat as its water flows through the exchange tank, then that heat must be replenished by a heater to keep the holding tank at 60°C.

2-F If the liquid of System 1 flows more slowly, it will have more time to cool, so the temperature at the exit point (Point A) would be lower.

3-B Looking at the chart for Experiment 1, the temperature at Point D for 1" glass pipe is 21°C and for 2" glass pipe is 23°C. If the pipe were 3" wide, it is likely that the temperature would increase another 2°C, giving a reading of 25°C.

4-H This question requires that you carefully follow the methodology of the experiment. In Experiment I, water is pumped counter clockwise through System I. Notice that in Experiment II, it states water is pumped clockwise through System I. The data point, therefore, is found in the Experiment II results.

5-D The holding tank of System 1 starts out warmer because both experiments show System 1 losing heat between Points A and B. We can deduce that System 2 is always colder than System 1 because, in both experiments, System 2 gains heat between Points C and D. Since Points A and B show a lower temperature, cooling takes place in the exchange tank (so III is true). This means that cooler water is being returned to the holding tank of System 1, and warmer water is being returned to System 2. Cooling must also take place in the holding tank of System 2 for it to remain 20°C when warmed water is entering it from the exchange tank.

6-H The heat generated in the System 1 holding tank dissipates as it moves through the pipes in the transfer tank. Some of this heat will invariably dissipate into the environment. Insulating the transfer tank will help prevent much of this heat loss and improve the overall transfer of heat from the System 1 pipes to the water in the transfer tank.

Passage II (Data Representation)

Figure 1 is a graph with six shapes used to represent quantities. The wider a vertical cross section is, the greater quantity it indicates. The figures are divided into three ages of a lake: young, mature, and old. To better illustrate the three phases, the figures have gray, white, and black portions. The information is not about one specific lake; it is based on the study of many lakes.

7-D The key words in the question are "total number of organisms." The top shape in Figure 1 represents the total number of organisms. Beginning at the left, the shape gradually gets wider during the young portion, remains the same during the mature age, and then swells during old age. D is the only answer that describes this relationship.

8-G The bottom of Figure 1 shows "Lake Age" between two arrows. Graphs usually have the horizontal or vertical directions labeled. The horizontal labeling is usually at the bottom but can also appear at the top. The vertical labeling can be on the right or the left of the graph.

9-D This question requires that you compare one shape (rate of nutrient recycling) to the horizontal axis (age of the lake). The words "rate of nutrient recycling" call your attention to the second shape from the top. You do not need to know what "nutrient recycling" means, but rather, how to interpret the shape. Since the shape gets wider from left to right, the rate goes up as the lake gets older.

10-J Information can be represented in different ways. Figure 1 has information represented visually. Of Graphs I, II, III, and IV, only one correctly represents the relationship between lake age and variety of life. Graph II shows a sharp increase, followed by a long stable period, and then a sharp decrease. Graph I begins with a decrease. Graphs III and IV begin with an increase and never decrease.

11-C To answer this question, you need to look at the bottom two shapes of Figure 1 and find any place where the two shapes have the same width. Next, you determine which of statements I, II, and III are true and which are false. I is true, so every possible correct answer will have I in it; thus, you can ZAP D. II is false, so you can ZAP B. III is true, so you can ZAP A.

Passage III (Conflicting Viewpoints)

12-H The scientists of Group 1 need to find proof of two things to support that their theory is a viable cause of mass extinctions and, therefore, can be applied to other mass extinctions: 1) proof of a meteor collision at the end of the Cretaceous; and 2) proof that dust thrown up from a meteor collision could cause a catastrophic global winter. H is possible proof that a meteor did strike at the end of the Permian. Knowing this, Group 1 could argue that the causes of the Permian and Cretaceous extinctions were similar.

13-B Group 1 needs to prove that dust thrown up from a meteor collision could create a global winter. B is correct because forest fires also produce a lot of smoke and dust. If these could lower global temperatures, then it is very likely that a much greater disaster, like a meteor collision, could lower temperatures enough to create a global winter.

14-H Group 2 makes the claim that dinosaurs on the Australian continent were already subject to—and able to survive—harsh winter conditions and therefore would not have been affected by climatic change brought about by a meteorite strike. This assumption ignores the possibility that winter-like conditions would have been greatly exacerbated by such an impact. Winter conditions would have been much longer and harsher than those to which the animals and plants were adapted.

15-B Group 1's theory is that meteoric dust and debris filtered out the sunlight, killing plant life and the dinosaurs. A new discovery of deposits left by an extraterrestrial object adds nothing to this theory.

16-F The first paragraph explains that both groups of scientists are trying to explain why so many species became extinct at the end of the Cretaceous Period. Both groups agree that many large animals became extinct (F). They do not agree *why* they became extinct (G, H, and J)

17-A Group 1 insists that all dinosaurs were wiped out by the mass extinction. This would include the dinosaurs of the Australian continent, which Group 2 admits were extinct by the end of the Cretaceous. This means that the Australian dinosaurs could have been killed as a result of Group 1's meteor impact.

18-G The last sentence of the passage says that Group 2 believes that the mass extinction by the end of the Cretaceous Period was gradual. Only Line G shows a gradual decline in numbers. Incidentally, Line H represents Group 1's theory of sudden mass extinction at the end of the Cretaceous Period.

Science Answer Review Workout B

Passage I (Research Summaries)

Experiments 1 and 2 are attempts to study the relationship between magnetism, motion, and electricity. The first experiment establishes that electricity is generated when a magnet moves through a wire. Experiment 2 determines how the speed of the magnet affects the amount of electricity produced.

1-C Experiment 1 is *qualitative* because it deals with what qualities are discovered when you pass a magnet through a wire coil. It was discovered that passing a magnet through a coil of wire produces electricity. Experiment 2 is *quantitative* because it determines what quantities of electricity are produced. For example, 4.43 amperes is the quantity produced when the magnet is allowed to freely fall through the coil.

2-G The diagram of Experiment 2 shows the magnet on a string that is fed through two pulleys, and a weight on the other end of the string attached to a hook. The more weight you add to the hook, the slower the magnet will fall.

3-B The chart shows how much electricity is produced using different weights on the hook. The heavier the weight, the slower the magnet moves through the coil. Since the greatest weight (0.8 kg) resulted in the least amperes, and the least weight (no weight added), yielded the greatest amperes, you can deduce that the faster the velocity (or speed) of the magnet, the greater the current generated will be.

4-G Hypotheses are based upon hypothetical deductive reasoning — what we can deduce from the interaction of our experimental variables. The two variables being explored here are the relationship between the velocity of the magnet (the independent variable) and the current generated (the dependent variable).

5-D The weights on the hook are an attempt to regulate how fast the magnet falls through the hoop. By using the same weight, the experiment is consistent. Every time the magnet falls through the hoop with a .4 kg weight, the experimenter knows that the magnet is falling at the same rate of speed. However, the experimenter doesn't know exactly how fast the magnet is falling the moment it enters the hoop. Knowing how fast the magnet falls each time will improve the data.

6-F Power plants generate electricity by spinning huge coils through powerful magnetic fields at great speeds. Experiments 1 and 2 also generate electricity but on a much smaller scale. Since the experiment took place on the earth, we can conclude that it was not measurably affected by electrical fields in the earth and has little value for measuring such fields (G). Understanding how certain materials conduct electricity can be done with a more reliable (or consistent) power source, such as a battery (H). Devising a theory of magnetism would involve much more attention to how the magnet works than was shown in Experiments 1 and 2.

Passage II (Data Representation)

Graphs A, B, and C show the correlation between the increase of greenhouse gases (CO_2 and methane) over the years 1850 and 1990 and the increase in average temperatures for those same years. Graph A has a horizontal line drawn through the middle that represents the average temperature measured between 1950 and 1980. Note that the years are labeled in 20-year intervals and that CO_2 is carbon dioxide.

7-D You need to examine each answer and see if it corresponds to increases and decreases on the graphs. Only Graphs B and C show increases. Since the question has a negative twist, asking which does *not* show an increase, you must look at Graph A, where decreases in mean temperatures are shown for the years 1900–1910, 1940–1950, and 1955–1970. Only 1900–1910 is offered as an answer.

8-H The mean temperatures for each of the years sampled are represented by the dots and NOT by the curved line. The vertical line between 1910 and 1930 stands for 1920, where a dot is the closest of the four choices to the horizontal line representing the mean temperature between 1950 and 1980.

9-C The curved lines do not represent data but assumptions and trends. You need to compare the answer choices to the places they refer to on the graphs and find years cited in the four answer choices that do not have any dots plotted. Graph C, representing methane, shows no dots between 1960 and 1970.

10-F Looking at Graph B, you see that the concentration of CO_2 was greater in 1980 than in 1850, so the correct answer will show the dark bar as being greater. This eliminates answers G and H, where the light bar for 1850 is greater. Answer J is tempting because Graph B places the concentration in 1980 several times higher than 1850. It is important to realize that the bottom of Graph B begins at 280 parts per million. If Graph B were drawn so that it started at 0 parts per million, the difference between 1850 and 1980 would look like the bar graph in F. It's as though the graphs have only enough room for the tips of the icebergs.

11-C On all three graphs, the lines drawn among the points indicate trends. You need to follow the line for each and extend it to the end of each graph. Choices A, B, and D would reverse the upward trend seen in the data. Only C continues this upward trend. Be sure you're reading closely: While a reading of −0.1 is possible, −1 (B) is extremely unlikely, as changes in previous years were never as great as a full degree in either direction.

Passage III (Research Summaries)

12-F You need to examine each of the four choices, deciding which conclusion is true and which three are false. When the decreased diameter was lowered one meter in Experiment 3, the water pressure increased. Answers G and H are wrong because each implies that narrowing the tube and lowering the tube had the same effect on water pressure. In truth, narrowing the tube decreased the pressure, and lowering the tube increased the pressure. F is correct because a decrease in diameter caused the water pressure in the narrow part of the tube to decrease (Experiment 2). J is wrong; although the two factors had opposite effects on water pressure, the lowered elevation did not cancel out the effect of the narrowed tube.

13-D This is a question that can be answered using common sense. Choice A can be ZAPPED because we are told that the air pressure outside each of the three vertical tubes is the same. B and C can be ZAPPED because the volume of the water in the tube neither increases nor decreases at any point. D is the only choice left.

Science Answer Review Workout B

14-J We are told that the fluid pressure in the middle tube is the lowest of the three. We are also told that the velocity is higher in the middle tube. The only answer that expresses this relationship is J: As the velocity increases, fluid pressure decreases. You may already know this principle. But if it wasn't already supported by the text, you'd be wrong to choose it.

15-B The answer can be found by taking the difference between the water levels for the middle tube of the second and third experiments:

30 cm − 22.5 cm = 7.5 cm

16-G The hypothetical experiment is like Experiment 3, except that the glass tube is raised a meter instead of lowered a meter. When the tube was lowered one meter, the water level rose 7.5 cm; if the tube were to be raised one meter, the water level should decrease by 7.5 cm.

22.5 − 7.5 = 15 cm

17-A Capping the tubes stops the water flow. As a result, the fluid velocity is irrelevant. Since the atmospheric pressure and the fluid volume would remain constant, the answer is A.

Passage IV (Data Representation)

18-J F, G, and H are all independent variables being tested in the experiments. Only J, the number of organisms per gram, represents the dependent or responding variable, that which is being measured in each experiment.

19-B B accurately describes the data trend seen for staphylococci grown at 95 °F on chicken à la king. A, C, and D are false statements not supported by the data.

20-H As in question 19, you must look at one chart (salmonellae for chicken à la king) and find the graph between days 1 and 2 to see which line shows the greatest upward increase. This occurs at 50°F.

21-A The experiment reveals only the growth rates of salmonellae and staphylococci when stored at various temperatures up to 5 days. Answers B, C, and D all assume that a low growth rate of these bacteria means the food is safe. A safe level of bacteria is not given in this experiment.

22-J Neither graph shows the results past the fifth day, so you will need to project trends into the sixth day. By locating the data for the four given temperatures, you can see that the chicken à la king at 48 degrees will be most likely to yield the highest salmonella per gram if the trends continue.

Science Answer Review
Workout C

Passage I (Conflicting Viewpoints)

Your clue that this passage is the one on conflicting viewpoints is that the opinions of two people are represented in the paragraphs labeled Geologist 1 and Geologist 2. A viewpoint can only be present where people are cited, and viewpoints cannot conflict unless there is more than one person involved.

1-B   Geologist 1 supports the statement that there are no deep earthquakes by saying that the techniques for measuring earthquakes are inaccurate. However, Geologist 1 offers no proof of this. Answer B would be the proof needed to show that the measurements were inaccurate.

2-J   This question has a negative twist in the word "contradict," so you need to look for the statement that definitely has a negative effect on Geologist 1's theory. Geologist 1 insists that "the earth is plastic below a depth of from 60 to 100 kilometers and *cannot fracture.*" J contradicts this assertion, suggesting that asthenosphere can break like a brittle solid.

3-A   Geologist 2 claims that deep earthquakes are caused by plates of lithosphere that have been pushed down into the asthenosphere by other plates of lithosphere. This could only happen where at least two lithosphere plates intersect.

4-F   The second paragraph says that seismic data collected over 85 years suggest that earthquakes have occurred at depths above 50 to over 600 km. Although it isn't stated, we can assume that most scientists do not dispute this 85 years' worth of data. Geologist 1 claims that this data is wrong because it doesn't work with Geologist 1's theory. This is not a good enough reason to reject 85 years of data.

5-B   Graph II is the only graph suggesting that no earthquakes occur at depths lower than 100 km. According to Geologist 1, there should be no earthquakes below 100 km because material that deep is plastic and cannot fracture.

6-H   Geologist 1 insists that ALL material in the asthenosphere is plastic and flexible. In this use, *plastic* means that a substance can be molded and bent. Geologist 1 does not state that lithosphere can be in the asthenosphere. For lithosphere to be in the asthenosphere, this lithosphere must become plastic. According to Geologist 1, the same forces that give the asthenosphere plasticity, would also affect any plates of lithosphere that got into the asthenosphere.

7-C   The scientists agree that earthquakes result from the fracturing of the lithosphere.

Passage II (Research Summaries)

8-J   Group A represents the control group for this experiment. Controlled experiments require that both the control group and experimental group be treated as identically as possible. F, G, and H are true statements. J introduces additional variables into the experiment (age and sex) making this a false statement.

9-D   Group B shows that streptozotocin induces symptoms that resemble diabetes. Group C also received streptozoticin, but didn't show the same symptoms because they also received insulin. The insulin given to Group C reduced the symptoms shown in Group B.

10-G   This question closely resembles the previous question. Group A is the control group: normal rats showing no symptoms and receiving no drugs. Group C received drugs to induce diabetes-like symptoms but had these symptoms reduced by another drug.

Science Answer Review Workout C

11-D If the effect of streptozotocin on rats resembles that of diabetes in humans, then the data in the chart show three symptoms: loss of weight, increase in blood sugar, and decrease in the size of fat cells. Only loss of weight is offered as an answer.

12-G The rats of Group B show the strongest symptoms of diabetes and were injected with streptozotocin only.

13-C A, B, and D are all relevant questions, but they do not build upon data seen in the experiment. Only C is supported by the experimental results.

Passage III (Data Representation)

14-G The column "Salt Filtered from the Water" shows how much of each salt did *not* dissolve. All 10 grams of the sodium chloride sample dissolved, while only 0.5 grams of silver chloride and 1.4 grams of barium nitrate dissolved. Therefore, sodium chloride is more soluble than the other two salts.

15-C Anytime you increase temperature, you increase atomic motion, which increases solubility.

16-F To compute the solubility of silver chloride, you must subtract 9.5 grams (filtered from the water) from the original amount of 10 grams. 0.5 grams dissolved in 1 liter of water, so the solubility of silver chloride is 0.5 grams per liter.

17-A If sodium chloride is 20 times as soluble as barium nitrate, multiply 20 times the solubility of barium nitrate to get the solubility of sodium chloride.

solubility of barium nitrate = 1.4 grams per liter
$$\times\ 20$$
solubility of sodium chloride = 28 grams per liter

So, if 20 grams of sodium chloride was added to 1 liter of water, all of it would dissolve with 0 grams recovered.

18-H Since solubility is determined by how many grams dissolve per liter of water, this rate will not change when less water is used. Less salt will dissolve in less water, but the amount per liter will remain constant.

Science Answer Review
Workout D

Passage I (Data Representation)

1-A   This question has a negative twist, asking which is *not* supported. This type of question often requires that you examine each answer choice against the chart to see which are true and which are not. A is not supported; males and females both spend a lot of time foraging (brick, gray) as shown on the chart. B is supported because male traveling (black) is larger in most columns than female traveling (zigzag). C is supported because resting (slash) is smaller in most columns for males than for females. D is supported because female foraging (brick) is smallest during the afternoon.

2-F   This question has a negative twist, asking during which hour the chimpanzees are least likely to be resting. The symbol (slash), which indicates time spent resting for males and females, is the smallest in the column representing 0700.

3-D   If you look at the column for 1500, you will see that female foraging is less than male foraging. The same is true at 1600: females foraged less than males. At 1700, females foraged more; at 1800, females and males foraged the same amount of time. The male foraging behavior is graphed as a straight, horizontal line, and the segmented line shows whether females foraged more or less than the males for each time period. If you keep in mind "less, less, more, same," you will see that only D shows the female foraging to be less, less, more, same for the four hours plotted. Another way to approach this type of problem is to look for the most obvious difference in the chart (often the largest or smallest difference). Then find which graph matches that point(s). You can then quickly ZAP any graph that doesn't match those points.

4-J   This question requires you to carefully examine the data presented in the graph. F, G and H can be eliminated; all represent false statements not supported by the data presented. Only J represents a true statement based on the data presented.

5-C   For this question, you need to examine each of the answer choices, determining true from false conclusions. Choice A is false because resting (slash for both females and males) only decreases during the afternoon for males. B is false because resting (slash) is at its peak for both males and females in the afternoon. C is true. D is false because foraging (brick) decreases during the afternoon for females between 1200 and 1500.

Passage II (Research Summaries)

6-H   According to the chart for endothelial cells (Results of Experiment 1), the highest concentration of histamine is 10^{-3}, and the amount of HRP taken up at this concentration is 6.00 micrograms. Note that with negative exponents, 10^{-3} is greater than 10^{-4}.

7-B   As the concentration of histamine increases from 0 to 10^{-3} micrograms per milliliter, the amount of protein absorbed by the two types of cells increases. This is a positive effect: an increase in histamine causes an increase in HRP protein being taken up. The word *negligible* means *insignificant*. This is an example of how understanding college-level words is important the ACT and SAT, even though both claim not to put an emphasis on higher-level vocabulary. If you don't know the meaning of words like this, start studying college-level words now.

8-G   The correct answer must be based on the results of the experiments. Experiments 1 and 2 show that histamines have an effect on how much HRP is taken up by cells. However, HRP is not mentioned in the descriptive information as having any relationship with hardening of the arteries. The first sentence explains that lipids are involved. The scientist is assuming that HRP and lipids are taken up by cells in the same way.

Science Answer Review Workout D

9-D You need to find on each graph two levels of HRP that are close in quantity. 6.00 for endothelial cells and 5.80 for smooth muscle cells are closest, and their histamine concentrations are 10^{-3} and 10^{-4}.

10-G The question requires that you look at the values for 0 histamine concentration in both charts. In both cases, the cells still took up small amounts of HRP.

11-D For this question, you need to examine each answer choice to see if it is supported by the data. Since the question has a negative twist in asking which is *not* supported, it helps to label the answers *true* or *false* as you go through them. Choice A is true: values of HRP found in smooth muscle cells are greater for equal concentrations of histamine. Choice B is true: compare 1.12 for 0 histamine and 2.63 for 10^{-6}. Choice C is true: *permeability* means the ability of a cell to be penetrated. If the cell walls were not permeable, then HRP wouldn't be able to get in at all. Since greater levels of HRP are found when histamine is used, histamine increases the permeability. Choice D is false because the charts show that smooth muscle cells take up more HRP than endothelial cells, not less. Compare 1.12 for smooth muscle cells and 0.16 for endothelial cells.

Passage III (Research Summaries)

12-J Figure 1 shows the following results of Experiment 1: as time passed, fewer bacteria survived, so time may have had an effect. Higher temperatures made the number of survivors smaller, so temperature may have had an effect. And, since agent X was applied to *all* tests in Experiment 1, we don't know if it had an effect or not. We can only assume that agent X may have affected the survival of *E. coli*.

13-B To determine whether agent X affects the survival of *E. coli*, an experimenter needs to try different amounts of agent X, keeping temperature, time, and age of *E. coli* constant. If you discovered that fewer bacteria survived when you used more agent X, you could deduce that agent X aids in killing *E. coli*.

14-H Agent X is known to kill some types of bacteria, and it is used in Experiment 1. Because Experiment 1 is testing both the effect of temperature and agent X on *E. coli* one can not conclude from the graph which variable is responsible for the trend seen. Obviously a similar test needs to be conducted testing temperature and agent X separately.

15-B Experiments 2 and 3 were about the destruction of bacterial spores, so you need to study Tables 1 and 2. Agent X was not used in either experiment. Knowing this, you could eliminate answer choices A, C, and D because they all include agent X (1). All the spores were killed at 130°C in moist heat (Experiment 2) while many were still alive at 130°C in dry heat (Experiment 3). Increased temperature, *not* decreased temperature, killed more spores in both experiments.

16-F For this question, you need to examine the choices and see which are true and which are false. In Table 1, you see that at 110°C it took 1 minute to destroy *Bacillus anthracis*, so F is true. In Table 2, soil spores fared best, so they are *not* relatively vulnerable to dry heat (G). No experiment tested the effect of moist heat on *E. coli* (H), a vegetative, non spore-forming bacteria. Although some spores in Experiment 3 did survive temperatures at 180°C, we do not know if any would survive at higher than 180°C (J), since no higher temperatures were used.

17-C This problem is simple. Experiment 2 involves moist heat. Experiment 3 involves dry heat. ZAP A, B, and D. These organisms were in both experiments. *Clos. sporogenes* were in Experiment 2 only.

Passage IV (Data Representation)

The schematic diagram shows the interaction between four machines: compressor, boiler, turbine, and condenser. Points 1, 2, 3, and 4 are places between each machine where pressure and volume measurements have been taken and are displayed in Graph A. The highest and lowest pressures are recorded as P_1 and P_2. Graph B shows how the difference between the highest and lowest pressure readings affects the efficiency of the work output. The system is most efficient when the amount of work output is closest to the amount of work input.

18-G   The answer is found in Graph A, where pressure and volume are plotted. Pressure is shown on the vertical line, where a rising or falling line indicates a change in pressure. Where the graph is horizontal, no change in pressure occurs. There is no change in pressure between points 1 and 4 and points 2 and 3. Looking at the schematic diagram, you see that the boiler and condenser are between these points.

19-C   All answer choices can be found in Graph A, where you will see changes of pressure between points 1 and 2 and points 3 and 4. There is an increase in pressure between 1 and 2 (follow the arrows) and a decrease between 3 and 4. On the schematic diagram, the compressor and turbine are between points 1 and 2 and points 3 and 4. Between 3 and 4, work is yielded as the pressure decreases.

20-J   Graph A shows the change in specific volume on the horizontal axis. The greatest jump is between points 1 and 4 which, according to the schematic, is the condenser.

21-A   The question asks about efficiency, which is plotted on the horizontal axis of Graph B. The ratio between two equal values will be 1, so look for 1 on the horizontal axis to find its corresponding efficiency value. The line shows an efficiency (on the vertical axis) of 0.

22-G   You must understand the meaning of $\frac{P_1}{P_2}$ in the horizontal axis of Graph B. Efficiency increases (as shown by the rising curve) as $P_1 \div P_2$ becomes a greater number. P_1 and P_2 stand for numbers that measure pressure. To raise the value of $P_1 \div P_2$, you need to either increase P_1 or decrease P_2. Only decreasing P_2 is offered as an answer choice.

Science Answer Review Workout E

Passage I (Data Representation)

1-B Look at the chart for River B and decide which one material was in greatest quantity. The graph that occupies the largest area represents the material in greatest quantity. If you counted the rectangles, fine sand covers 19 full rectangles, whereas medium sand occupies 14, and silt, 13.

2-H For this question, you need to examine each answer choice and decide if it is true or false, based on the data. The correct choice will be true. F is false: if finer particles were lighter than water, the graphs for these particles would get wider near the top. G is false for the same reason. The graphs for coarse and medium sand get wider near the bottom. H is true: clay and silt are the finer particles. Their graphs do not get as wide near the bottom, because they are evenly distributed throughout the depth of the river. J is false because the graphs for coarser particles get wider near the bottom.

3-C Anything that is heavier than water would tend to sink, so the greatest concentrations would be found at the bottom. All the sedimentary materials do this to some degree. Note that if the water weren't moving, all materials would have a chance to sink to the bottom.

4-F All of the river sediments are heavier than water. This is shown in each graph's tendency to be wider at the bottom. If the sediments were allowed to settle, they would all end up in layers on the bottom.

5-D Differing turbulence, volume of water, and depth of the river would affect how much each type of material is churned up in the water. However, the *proportion* of materials would be determined by the soil type found on the bottom of each river.

Passage II (Conflicting Viewpoints)

6-H A careful reading of both viewpoints reveals that both scientists are explaining why the Viking probe recorded no signs of life on Mars. Scientist 1 claims that the probe's search was not thorough; Scientist 2 claims that the probe found no traces of life because there is no life on Mars. Since both scientists are explaining why the Viking probe revealed no signs of life, they agree that no life was found on Mars.

7-B Scientist 1 argues that Mars is a likely candidate for the existence of life because its "landscape is quite similar to that of the Earth" and has "volcanoes, canyons, and polar ice caps." In citing this as a reason, Scientist 1 is suggesting that similar conditions in the environment could result in similar life forms.

8-F Scientist 1 insists that further work must be done to find life on Mars. He or she is insisting that life is there, but we haven't found it yet. Scientist 1 is operating on the assumption that life must be there because it is theoretically possible. The fact that life is theoretically possible on Mars is not proof that it actually exists.

9-D The question is, "Would the probe accurately detect life under conditions such as those found on Mars?" To test this, the probe should be used on a frozen desert region on Earth, where scientists know that it should find some traces of life.

10-H Scientist 1 argues that Martian lifeforms may be so different from forms of life on Earth that it would be difficult to know what to look for. Under these circumstances, Scientist 1 would not support looking for similar lifeforms.

11-A The evidence of drastic climatic changes on Mars suggests that if life had developed, it may have been destroyed by one of these major changes in climate. Therefore, scientists would be justified in looking for signs of life destroyed by drastically changing climates.

12-G Neither scientist would say that lifeforms exist only on Earth. Scientist 1 says, "it seems probable that life does exits there [Mars]." Scientist 2 says, "There may be other forms of life somewhere in the universe. . . ."

Passage III (Research Summaries)

13-C Only light wavelengths emitted by the gas will get through the two slits and enter the prism. Wavelengths not emitted by the gas will show as black areas on the line spectra.

14-J Only J is a true statement. F, G, and H are all false statements not supported by the experimental data.

15-A According to the line spectrum emitted by mercury (Experiment 1), the visible light bands seem concentrated near the blue and green wavelengths. Under these circumstances, it is logical that light emitted from mercury will appear blue and green.

16-J In the line spectra for Experiment 1, the white bands are wavelengths that are emitted when each of the gases is electrified. In Experiment 2, the black bands are spectra that are absorbed when white light travels through the gases.

The line spectrum emitted by mercury shows several bands ranging in size from 250 nm to 700 nm. The line spectrum absorbed by mercury shows only one band at about 230 nm. The two spectra have no wavelengths in common, so mercury absorbs none of the spectrum that it emits as an electrified gas.

The line spectrum emitted by sodium has some lines in common with the line spectrum absorbed by sodium. These bands range from 250 nm to 350 nm. Sodium absorbs some, but not all, of the wavelengths it emits as an electrified gas.

17-D According to the line spectra of Experiment 2, certain wavelengths of light are absorbed by certain elements. The theory suggests that each wavelength of light corresponds to a certain energy level, so certain elements will absorb light at certain energy levels.

18-G An application uses the results of an experiment to answer new questions. Experiment 1 resulted in the discovery of the line spectra of two gases, mercury and sodium. The only choice that uses this knowledge is G. The other choices depend on knowledge that Experiment 1 *did not* yield, so you can *ZAP* all of them.

Science Answer Review Workout F

Passage I (Data Representation)

1-B Compare each answer choice against the graph. A is *not* true: the energy increase is shown by the curve that begins at 5 kJ, jumps to 8, then descends to 3. This is not a constant energy increase. B *is* true: the intermediate complex is formed at 8 kJ, but has lost 5 kJ by the time it has turned into E + F. C is *not* true because the energy level starts at 5 and ends at 3. D is *not* true because the energy level increases by 2 kJ when E + F is changed into A + B.

2-J The curve in the chart shows the energy level. The far left shows the start of the reaction with an energy level of 5 kJ; the far right shows the end is at 3 kJ, which is 2 kJ lower than the beginning.

3-C The path of the curve is reversible. The forward reaction is from left to right; the reverse, from right to left. In both directions, the reactions begin with an energy gain until they reach 8 kJ, at which point they lose energy.

4-G If the vertical and horizontal axes remain unchanged, the reverse reaction would be shown as a left/right mirror image of the graph in Figure 1.

5-B It is important to remember that this question is asking about the reverse reaction. The largest change in energy is a 5 kJ change when E + F change into IC.

Passage II (Research Summaries)

6-J This question tests your knowledge of scientific procedures. The instructor assumed that the rods would expand at a constant rate. You know this because the instructor took only two measurements of the length of the rod—one before and one after heating. Had the instructor not assumed this, he or she would have measured the time and temperature and measured the rod at various points in time as the rod expanded.

7-D Look at the two charts: both charts show in the last column the total change in length of the rods. In both experiments, the rod that expanded most in Experiment 1 was also the rod that expanded most in Experiment 2. The rods were consistent in their expansion, so the projections from the two rods support each other.

8-J This question tests your knowledge of common safety procedures in a science experiment. Any *flammable* liquid (which means the same thing as "*inflammable* liquid") must be safely contained. You need to be familiar with laboratory procedures for the ACT Science Test.

9-A This is a division problem. Look at the bottom row in the chart for Experiment 1. A 100-cm rod expanded .175 cm. If the rod had been 25 cm, or $\frac{1}{4}$ as long, you could figure this out by dividing .175 by 4:

.175 cm ÷ 4 = .04375 cm

Then round .04375 cm up to .044 cm.

10-G Anyone familiar with scientific principles could deduce that the expansion of metals is related to molecular activity, but the challenge is to examine the experiment and see if there is anything in the experiment that points to this conclusion. Neither experiment makes a connection between expansion and molecular activity.

11-C This question can be solved empirically. Looking at the net change on both charts, you see that metal X expanded approximately $\frac{3}{5}$ as much as zinc. This means that the coefficient of expansion for metal X would be about $\frac{3}{5}$ of the coefficient of expansion for zinc. Looking at the chart under question 11, you will see that 16.8 (for copper) is about $\frac{3}{5}$ of 26.28 (for zinc).

Passage III (Research Summaries)

12-H This question is very *ZAP-able*. Each graph line in the answer choices represents a column in Table 2. Looking at Table 2 for October, you can see the depth of frozen soil was 1 for each plot. Any correct graph will have all three lines beginning at 1, so you can *ZAP* F and G. Looking at the data for November, you will see that Plot 1 should be twice the values for Plots 2 and 3. Only Choice H shows one line at twice the number as the other two.

13-D In Table 1, you see that the greatest snow cover is in Plot 3, followed by Plot 2, then Plot 1. In Table 2, you see that the depth of frozen ground is greatest in Plot 1, followed by Plot 2, then Plot 3. Where the snow is thickest, the frozen ground is thinnest and vice versa.

14-F One logical conclusion is that the growth of hay would be depressed, as it was for other plants in Plot 1. But since this is not one of the choices, it seems more likely that the effect the activity will have on the hay cannot be determined. There is no proof that deep freezing would hinder the growth of hay, as we don't know what type of vegetation was growing in the test plots, and hay might respond differently than whatever was grown there previously.

15-A This question requires some insight into scientific procedures. A control needs to resemble the test plot in every way except for the one thing that is being tested. A control plot for a snowmobile-ridden hay field should be an identical hay field without snowmobile traffic.

16-H Plot 1 is the test plot, so the control plot should resemble Plot 1 as closely as possible. Plot 3 is not a very good control plot because it is in the forest and is quite different from the test plot.

17-D Examine each choice to find one that is true. Choice A is not true because the experiments do not show that decreased snowcover increased the freezing of plant seeds. Choice B is not true because it was not shown that the plot the snowmobiles ran on experienced a delayed thaw. Choice C is not true because Table 4 shows that Plot 1 never recovered to produce as much vegetation as Plots 2 and 3. Choice D is true: negative correlation means that as one thing increases the other decreases. As the depth of the frozen ground increased, the quantity of vegetation the following summer decreased.

Science Answer Review Workout F

Passage IV (Data Representation)

18-J It is important to realize that protons and neutrons are expressed as whole numbers, and, therefore, they can be plotted as exact points on a graph.

19-B Look at the graph at the intersection of 40 on the vertical scale and 51 on the horizontal scale. At this intersection is a black square, indicating that a nucleus with 40 protons and 51 neutrons exists and is stable. (Note that the passage describing the graph explains that black points denote stable nuclei.)

20-G On the graph, a line labeled N = Z shows where nuclei that have equal numbers of protons and neutrons would be plotted. Some with numbers below 10 exist, but as the numbers increase, the graph curves to the right, indicating that the number of neutrons exceeds the number of protons. So the number of protons (Z) divided by the number of neutrons (N) will be less than 1 for most nuclei.

21-A When a nucleus loses an alpha particle (alpha decay), it loses 2 protons and 2 neutrons. On the chart, the new nucleus would be lower and to the left of the old nucleus.

22-F A scientist is claiming that a stable nucleus (shown in black) can lose a proton without losing a neutron. The chart indicates that this could produce either a stable or unstable nucleus, depending on which nucleus loses the proton. If a stable nucleus loses only a proton, the resulting nucleus would be plotted one number lower on the chart. Some nuclei show unstable nuclei below them (clear); others show stable nuclei (black).

> The most exciting phrase to hear in science, the one that heralds the most discoveries, is not "Eureka!" (I found it!) but "That's funny…."
> —Isaac Asimov

Appendix D

Persuasive Argument Structures

Persuasive Argument Structures

As you practice for the enhanced essay—and write persuasive essays for school—try using any of these structures to organize your writing. Once you get comfortable with one or more of them, you'll find it easier to build a solid persuasive argument under the pressure of time. Remember, your goal should be to choose a structure that best suits your overall purpose.

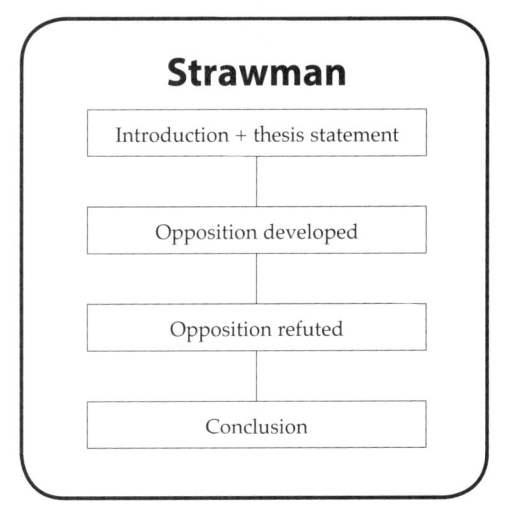

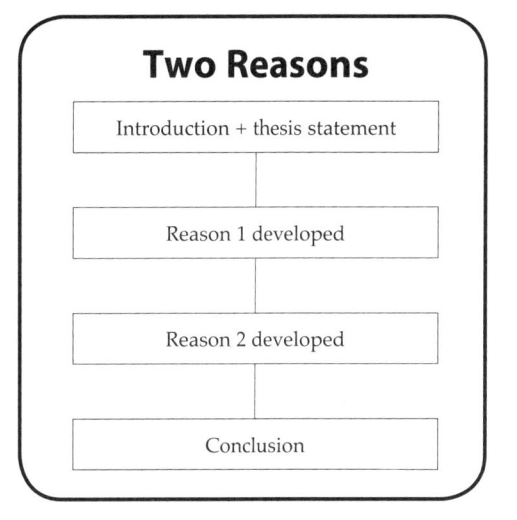

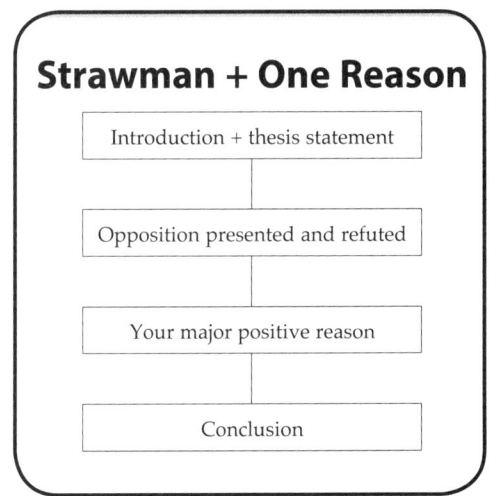

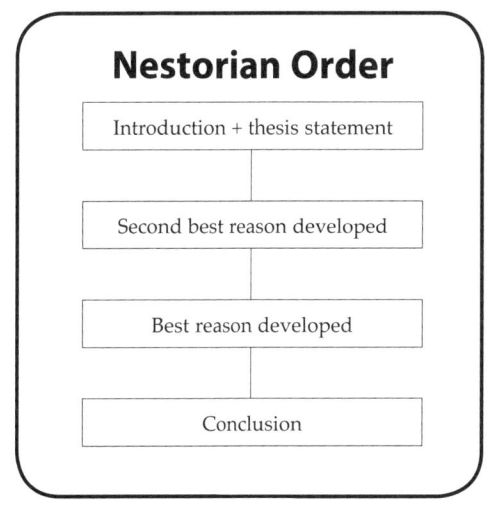

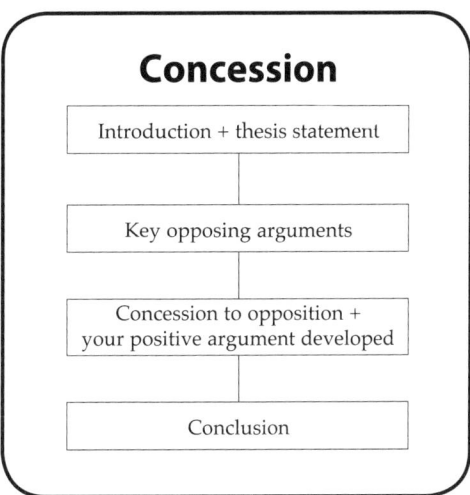

Strawman
- Introduction + thesis statement
- Opposition developed
- Opposition refuted
- Conclusion

Two Reasons
- Introduction + thesis statement
- Reason 1 developed
- Reason 2 developed
- Conclusion

Strawman + One Reason
- Introduction + thesis statement
- Opposition presented and refuted
- Your major positive reason
- Conclusion

Nestorian Order
- Introduction + thesis statement
- Second best reason developed
- Best reason developed
- Conclusion

Concession
- Introduction + thesis statement
- Key opposing arguments
- Concession to opposition + your positive argument developed
- Conclusion

Doorway to College™ Foundation

PRODUCT GUIDE

STUDY SKILLS
- Study Smart! Classes
- Study Smart! Study Skills Recording 
- Study Skills for Classroom Tests E-book

TEST PREP
- ZAPS ACT Seminars, Webinars, and Recordings 
- ZAPS PSAT/SAT Seminars, Webinars, and Recordings 
- ACT Subtest Intensive Instructional Videos
- ZAPS Online ACT or SAT Practice Test
- ZAPS College Vocabulary Challenge
- Tame Test Anxiety: Confidence Training for Teens 
- Personal Best Test Training (PBTT) Seminars and Webinars

COLLEGE PREP
- Writing an Exceptional College Entrance Essay E-book
- Interviewing: In the Hot Seat E-book 
- College Applications E-book
- Making the Most of Your College Visit E-book
- College Admissions Essay E-book  
- Kickstart to College Workshops 1 + 2

STUDENT ATHLETE
- #1: Goal Setting for Student Athletes E-book
- #2: The Division Decision E-book
- #3: The Road to Playing College Sports E-book
- #4: How to Succeed as a College Athlete E-book

*Use promo code **doorway2college** to receive a 10% discount on digital products!*

877-927-8378 prep@doorwaytocollege.com Doorway to College @Doorway2College www.doorwaytocollege.com